i love
meatballs!

i love
meatballs!

RICK RODGERS

Photography by Ben Fink

Andrews McMeel
Publishing, LLC

Kansas City • Sydney • London

Andrews McMeel Publishing, LLC
an Andrews McMeel Universal company
1130 Walnut Street, Kansas City, Missouri 64106

www.andrewsmcmeel.com

11 12 13 14 15 WKT 10 9 8 7 6 5 4 3 2 1

ISBN: 978-1-4494-0784-1

Library of Congress Control Number: 2011921503

Design: Holly Ogden
Photography: Ben Fink
Food Stylist: Susan Ottaviano
Prop Stylist: Dani Fisher

www.rickrodgers.com

Attention: Schools and Businesses

Andrews McMeel books are available at quantity
discounts with bulk purchase for educational,
business, or sales promotional use. For information,
please e-mail the Andrews McMeel Publishing Special
Sales Department: specialsales@amuniversal.com

contents

acknowledgments

When you look at a cookbook, you see the author's byline. This isn't fair, as a cookbook is hardly a solo effort. Many talented, hardworking people assisted me in the creation of this book. Countless hundreds of meatballs were consumed in the name of research!

First of all, thanks to my fellow meatball lover and editor, Jean Lucas, for her dedication to the cause. I hope I've finally provided her with the perfect meatball recipe. Kirsty Melville, our intrepid leader at Andrews McMeel, also jumped on the meatball bandwagon, and she inspired us to think outside of the meatball box. Thanks to Holly Ogden for the vibrant book design, and to Tammie Barker for getting the word out.

This book is another happy collaboration between photographer Ben Fink and me. Thank you, Ben, for always making my food look so luscious. Ben's crews are always made up of the best people in the business, and food stylist Susan Ottaviano and prop stylist Dani Fisher continued the tradition.

In my kitchen, very little would get accomplished without the sister I never had, Diane Kniss, who has cooked by my side for more years than we dare to count. And Patrick Fisher, taster extraordinaire, personally vetted all of the recipes in this book, and assured me that a freezer full of leftover meatballs is a dream come true. My friends and food professionals Carolyn Bánflavi and Diane Phillips, and Carolyn's husband, Gabor, contributed their best recipes and I appreciate their tasty input. My incomparable agent, Susan Ginsburg, generously offered her indispensable friendship and advice.

introduction

How can a food be comforting and retro, yet cutting-edge and hip all at the same time? The meatball has deftly managed this balancing act. Ever since humans discovered that chopping tenderized tough meat, and that rolling the mixture into balls made for a tasty and easy-to-eat way to cook them, meatballs have been served up by everyone from Italian grandmothers to of-the-moment chefs. *I Love Meatballs!* shares over fifty of my favorite recipes for the world's best meatballs for every occasion, from family meal to dinner party.

Like so many of us, my love affair with meatballs started at the family kitchen table. Every American family has a trustworthy meatball recipe, whether for spaghetti and meatballs, Swedish meatballs, or another specialty. And, even better, meatballs can be economical and relied upon to satisfy a hungry table of diners while staying within the tightest budget.

Every cuisine has its own version of meatballs. Greeks love their herb-seasoned *keftedes*. Latino cooks adore *albóndigas* as tapas or in soup. Germans can't live without *Kögisberger Klopse* (poached meatballs in a caper sauce). Nor would the Danes want to go too long without delicate veal-and-pork *frikadeller*. Swedish meatballs in a light brown sauce are just as popular here as they are in their native country!

Kofta (and similar-sounding words) means "meatball" to both Middle Eastern and Indian cooks, as the word comes from the Persian word for "to grind" and has traveled far and wide. Chinese cuisine features meatballs both small (as part of the dim sum menu) and large (lion's head). The Vietnamese serve meatballs on noodles or rice, or tucked into sandwiches.

Meatballs can be grilled and dipped, simmered and sauced, fried and nibbled. They can be retro (people make fun of the fifties' sweet-and-sour meatball until they try one) or upscale (try chopping the meat at home for truly remarkable meatballs), and used in soups, stews, sandwiches, and casseroles. And they are all here. While some cooks will argue that a meatball must have meat in the form of beef, pork, veal, or lamb, I have included some seafood- and poultry-based balls. Not only are they delicious, they are lighter than their red-meat cousins in all senses of the word, and that can be as welcome as the heartier versions. Meatball possibilities are virtually endless. However, I wanted to keep this book to the very best meatballs that you are likely to make.

These recipes are hand-picked, based on ones that I have savored in my kitchen, my friends' kitchens, and my travels.

Perhaps it is the meatball's status as a beloved comfort food that has made it the current star of restaurant menus. Many formerly haughty chefs realized that their profit margin would benefit from simpler fare, and the humble but reliably tasty meatball filled this need. (Not to mention that meatballs, with their many ethnic tangents and cooking techniques, can spark a chef's creativity.) I recently had high tea at one of the most exclusive hotels in Manhattan and saw meatball sliders on the menu, next to the cucumber sandwiches! One needs no better indicator of how meatballs have risen in stature.

Just because meatballs are a classic rustic dish, don't take them for granted. While there are some "fast and easy" meatball recipes, it is their nature to be carefully constructed. There are usually three components: a well-seasoned meat mixture, a tasty sauce (often long-simmered), and an appropriate starch to fill out the meal. I have included a detailed overview of meatball-making guidelines to give perfect results every time. So, push up your sleeves and get rolling!

MEATBALLS: INGREDIENTS AND TECHNIQUES

ingredients

Meatballs are made from ground meat (or seafood or poultry), with various ingredients added for flavoring, binding, and increasing the volume of the mixture. Understanding the roles played by the components can make the difference between a good meatball and a great one.

Meat is, of course, the foundation of meatballs, and is essential for taste, texture, and bulk. The vast majority of recipes in this book assume that the cook will use store-bought ground meat. Raw ground meat spoils fairly rapidly, so plan on using it to make and cook meatballs within 24 hours of purchase.

The ground meats used in this book are:

Ground beef is the main meat for many meatball recipes, used for its rich flavor. It is identified by the cut of meat used for grinding, the percentage of fat, or both. The most commonly sold grinds are ground sirloin (about 93 percent lean, 7 percent fat); ground round (85 percent lean, 15 percent fat); and ground chuck (80 percent lean, 20 percent fat). Generically named "hamburger" (also sometimes called "ground beef") is a mix of cuts with a fat content of more than 20 percent. The fat content is important. If the ground meat is too lean, as in the case of sirloin, the meatballs can end up resilient and dry. If the meat is too fatty (both chuck and hamburger, in my opinion), the meatballs and their sauce could have a greasy flavor, and the balls will shrink too much during cooking.

Ground round has the perfect ratio of lean meat to fat, resulting in tender, juicy meatballs. This grind also stands up well to long simmering. You can certainly substitute other cuts for reasons of personal taste, budget, or reducing fat content—just expect different results.

Buy ground beef that is cherry red with no signs of discoloration. Keep it tightly wrapped in its original packaging until you're ready to use it.

Ground veal yields the most delicate, tender meatballs. Veal contains high amounts of collagen and gelatin, connective tissue that melts during cooking to act as a binder and add an extra measure of juiciness to the meatballs. For these traits, ground veal is often combined with other meats. Only one kind of generic ground veal is sold, so don't look for a particular cut. The meat should be pale pink with white flecks and no tinge of dark red. It is not always available, so buy and freeze it when you see it at the market. If your butcher doesn't carry it, you can chop your own from boneless veal shoulder (see Chopping Your Own, page xix).

Ground pork, a flavor powerhouse, is used in many recipes. It is never lean and its fat content contributes to its tastiness. Like veal, only one kind of ground pork is available, so the cut isn't a consideration. Look for ground pork with a robust pink color and visible white flecks.

Ground lamb is not always sold at supermarkets but it is readily available at Middle Eastern and halal butchers. The lamb cuts usually used for grinding are highly marbled with fat and the meatballs will be full of flavor and juices, but perhaps too rich. Whenever possible, I go out of my way to purchase ground lamb at a local Middle Eastern butcher, where the meat is carefully trimmed and a little less fatty. For many cooks' tastes, it may be best to use half ground lamb and half lean ground sirloin to cut down on the fat. Ground lamb should be dark red-purple with white flecks.

Ground chicken has wonderful flavor, but it isn't particularly lean, as it is made from both dark and white meat, as well as the skin naturally attached to these cuts. The average fat content is about 10 percent, which makes it a little fattier than ground sirloin. I do not recommend ground chicken breast, which is available at some butcher shops, as it is very lean and makes dry meatballs.

Ground turkey is sold in a variety of permutations, so look carefully at the labeling to determine the fat content. The recipes in this book use lean ground turkey that is 93 percent lean with 7 percent fat, processed from a mix of dark and white meat with the attached skin. Extra-lean ground turkey breast meat is the leanest ground meat one can buy, at 1 percent fat—you will save calories but sacrifice flavor and moisture. Frozen turkey meat in a tube is mainly dark meat and its skin, and usually comes in at 15 percent fat (the same as ground round), but it has a strong flavor. Go with the standard ground turkey.

Seafood, which has a lower fat content than meat and poultry, makes delicious balls with reduced amounts of calories and fat. This is not a new idea, as Asian cooks have been making balls from ground fish and shellfish for centuries. Seafood is only sold whole so you'll need to finely chop it at home in a food processor, a simple chore, before using in meatballs.

Bread and Cracker Crumbs

All meatballs have some kind of binder, usually bread or cracker crumbs, to help the meat hold together. When the crumbs are moistened, they become sticky and act as a kind of glue. Be careful not to overdo the crumbs, as the meat's character should predominate—a bad meatball is one with its flavor masked with too many crumbs. Use just the amount needed to keep the meat mixture from falling apart, and no more. Yes, you can "stretch" the meat with more crumbs to get more servings, but that will be at the expense of flavor and texture.

Dried bread crumbs give meatballs a firm texture. They are available plain or with Italian seasonings such as herbs, garlic powder, and Romano cheese. Of course, plain crumbs are the most versatile, as seasonings can be easily added, but I know some cooks who prefer the convenience of the Italian-seasoned crumbs.

Fresh bread crumbs are used in many recipes, especially those of the Old World.

Fresh crumbs are usually soaked with milk to make a coarse paste that is easily distributed throughout the meat mixture during mixing, and makes for a softer, more tender meatball than one with dried crumbs. Sometimes the soaked crumbs are drained of excess milk, but often the milk is retained to add extra moisture to the meatballs.

Fresh bread crumbs are easily prepared. Just about any white bread will do—sandwich, crusty artisanal French or Italian, or even bagels. Do not use sourdough bread, as its tanginess is not always an appropriate addition. Some recipes call for a specific bread, such as rye, for its flavor.

I know many cooks who insist on using only the inner crumb of the bread for their crumbs, discarding the crust. (I have come across a recipe that starts with "Pull the soft crumbs from the inside of a stale roll and throw away the crust.") But, in truth, when the meatballs are formed and cooked, it is impossible to determine the inner crumb from the outer crust, and soaking softens the tougher crust, so I use both parts of the bread. But the choice is yours. Start with bread that is slightly stale—it should have a firm, not soft, texture. Tear the bread into 1- to 2-inch pieces and process for at least 30 seconds in a food processor or blender until fluffy and finely ground. Use immediately or transfer to a zippered plastic bag and freeze for up to 3 months. Do not bother to thaw the bread crumbs before using.

Cracker crumbs are also easily prepared, although you can buy prepared cracker meal, which is a little coarser than dried bread crumbs. Crackers can be processed into crumbs in a food processor, or placed in a plastic resealable bag and crushed with a rolling pin. Cracker crumbs, like dried bread crumbs, yield meatballs that are on the firm side.

Onions and Garlic

These members of the Allium family are used over and over as the main seasonings in meatballs. They must be in very small pieces, or their coarse texture will be an unpleasant contrast to the rest of the smooth meatball mixture.

In the case of onions, shredding is better than chopping, as shredding renders the onion into small pieces that virtually disappear into the meat. Simply shred the onion on the large holes of a box grater and add, along with any onion juices, to the meat mixture. To be sure that garlic is sufficiently fine, push the cloves through a garlic press.

In some recipes, the onion and garlic are cooked to soften them and mellow their flavors. In this case, finely chopping them is sufficient.

Eggs

Eggs are a common binder in meatballs, as the egg proteins firm up when heated. Use USDA large eggs.

Broth

Many meatballs are cooked in a broth-based liquid that is subsequently thickened into a flavorful sauce. Of course, the quality of the broth will affect the flavor of the sauce. Many cooks don't want to make homemade broth, and with so much canned broth available, who can blame them? However, not all broths are created equal.

Use reduced-sodium canned broth, as it has the best flavor. Canned chicken broth is a boon to the cook, and there are many good brands out there. However, I haven't found a canned beef broth that I really like—although when the meatballs are simmered in it, the flavor does improve. Nonetheless, I still recommend homemade beef broth for the best results. Just make it on a weekend afternoon at home and freeze to use later. Some upscale supermarkets sell fresh or frozen beef broth, which is a good, if pricey, alternative to the canned or homemade version.

Cheese

Shredded hard cheese, such as Parmesan and Romano, is an ingredient in many Italian-inspired meatball recipes. Always use the imported Italian varieties Parmigiano-Reggiano and Pecorino Romano. These are at their best when shredded just before using; if they are shredded too far ahead, they can dry out.

Salt and Pepper

Kosher salt, which is additive-free and has an unadulterated flavor, is the salt that many chefs and home cooks favor for savory cooking. Because the uncooked meat mixture contains raw eggs and meat, and therefore cannot be tasted to gauge its saltiness, I have provided a salt measurement for each meatball recipe that suits my standards. If you prefer to use plain (table) salt, iodized salt, or fine sea salt, these have smaller crystals than kosher salt, and measure differently. For every 1¼ teaspoons of kosher salt (to my taste, usually the amount needed to season 1 pound of ground meat), use 1 teaspoon of plain, iodized, or fine sea salt.

Pepper should be freshly ground from black peppercorns for the best flavor.

making the meatballs

Meatballs are simple and fun to make, but as it is for all cooking, a little attention to detail can make all the difference. Here are some tips and techniques that will guarantee excellent results every time.

Mixing It Up

The ingredients for the meatball mixture should be thoroughly combined, but not overhandled. If the mixture is compacted, the meatballs will be rubbery. When it comes to meatballs, your hands are the best mixing utensils. Just roll up your sleeves, wash your hands, and squish the ingredients together between your fingers until the mixture is homogenous. Squeamish cooks who do not like handling food with this level of intimacy can wear rubber or latex gloves. And a sturdy spoon will suffice to stir the ingredients together, but it is no replacement for your hands.

At this point, the meat mixture may seem soft and moist, but do not add more bread crumbs in an attempt to firm it up. (Some recipes, such as Danish Meatballs in Cream Sauce on page 78, are intentionally wet, as the liquid in the mixture yields especially tender meatballs.) A brief spell in the refrigerator will let the binding ingredients do their job, and it also stiffens the fat, facilitating rolling. Cover the bowl with plastic wrap and refrigerate the meat mixture for at least 15 minutes or up to 4 hours before forming the balls.

Shaping the Meatballs

As with mixing the meat mixture, once again your hands are the best tools for shaping meatballs. To keep the meat mixture from sticking, rinse your cleaned hands under cold running water before and during rolling. Some cooks I know prefer to oil their hands with either vegetable or olive oil instead. You can use a meatball shaper (also called a meatball scoop or baller), which looks like a pair of tongs with half-spheres at each end. They make uniform balls, but rinse or oil them frequently to keep the meat from sticking.

Each recipe provides the number of finished meatballs so you can estimate the amount of servings. People with big appetites may want four meatballs, while two and a half may be enough for daintier eaters. Portioning can be done with a little quick math. For example, many of the recipes make 18 meatballs. For easy portioning, divide the meat mixture in the bowl into thirds. Then, using a spoon, scoop six portions from each third, transferring the rough balls onto a baking sheet. I do this all by eye, and it goes quickly. (But if you like using a kitchen scale, go ahead.) Now rinse your hands with water and quickly smooth and roll the balls between your palms, taking care not to compact them.

If you have the time, cover and refrigerate the shaped meatballs to give them a final firming so they hold their shape better during cooking. This is optional unless the meatballs are so moist that a second chilling is a necessity (again, as with the Danish meatballs on page 78). In any case, the meatballs on the baking sheet can be covered with plastic wrap and refrigerated for up to 24 hours. This can be very helpful when you are making a large batch for a party.

cooking the meatballs

Pan-cooking is the traditional method for cooking meatballs, but it is hardly the only way. Each method here gives the finished meatballs a particular flavor and texture profile. There are times when you might want to swap one technique for another. Or, you can even combine methods. For example, meatballs can be grilled and then simmered to give a hint of smokiness to the sauce.

Pan-Cooking

Frying in a moderate amount of oil creates a browned crust on the meatball, increasing the meaty flavor and firming the surface. If a meatball mixture includes cheese (as many of the Italian-inspired ones do), the meatballs must be watched carefully during cooking to avoid burning.

A large nonstick pan does the best job of keeping sticking and burning at bay. But a sufficient amount of oil is still needed to help create the crust and act as added insurance against sticking. Cook the meatballs in batches, without crowding. If they are packed too closely in the pan, their steam will inhibit the browning. To reduce the mess on the stovetop

from sputtering oil, cover the skillet with a splatter shield. Adjust the heat as needed so the meatballs brown evenly and gently—you do not need to develop a thick crust—and turn them as soon as a thin crust develops on the undersides. This takes 6 to 8 minutes over medium heat. In most cases, the meatballs are going to be finished in a sauce, so they do not have to be cooked all the way through.

I have discovered an unorthodox utensil for turning meatballs: A thin metal fish spatula, with its slotted flexible blade and curved lip, is perfect for slipping under meatballs in the skillet. Just be careful not to scratch the nonstick surface with the metal spatula, or buy a nylon version to err on the side of caution.

As the meatballs are browned all over, return them to the baking sheet or a plate to await their final simmering. When browned bits are created in the pan, they should be used to build the flavor of the pan sauce. However, if, in spite of your best efforts, the bits become burned, throw them out and wipe out the pan with paper towels before proceeding.

Baking

Many a meatball lover's preferred method for browning is baking because it achieves results similar to pan-cooking, but without a messy stovetop. Place the meatballs on a lightly oiled half-sheet pan (a sturdy baking sheet measuring about 18 x 13 inches), on a standard rimmed baking sheet, or in a shallow roasting pan. You may also use a meatball baking pan, which has a metal rack with three troughs to hold the meatballs above the pan surface so the fat drips off. Bake the meatballs in a preheated 375°F oven for about 25 minutes, until they are lightly browned. If you wish, turn the meatballs halfway through the cooking time. (There is no need to turn the balls in a meatball pan, as the air circulates around the suspended balls and bakes them evenly.)

Braising

The secret to the meatballs of many an Italian *nonna* is braising, and other cuisines use the same method for extra-tender meatballs. The balls are not browned, but simply dropped into a simmering sauce, where the liquid surrounds and firms them. To help the meatballs keep their shape and to maintain the temperature of the simmering sauce, add the balls a few at a time to the pot. Some braised meatball recipes require long simmering, so use a thick-bottomed pot, such as a Dutch oven, or a flameproof casserole to avoid scorching.

Deep-Frying

For crispy meatballs, deep-frying is the way to go. They will also be very rich, so I usually reserve deep-frying for meatballs that will be served as appetizers. The key to deep-frying is that the oil should truly be *deep*. Skimping on the oil is a common mistake and leads to sogginess.

When hot oil is involved, you need to keep your wits about you. Before you get started, set yourself up so the process goes smoothly. Choose a heavy pot with at least a 3-quart capacity. Line a half-sheet pan or large baking sheet with a large brown paper bag, which is more absorbent than paper towels, and place near the stove. Preheat the oven to 200°F to keep the meatballs warm until serving. Have a wire spider (a large open-meshed skimmer) or a slotted spoon ready to transfer the meatballs from the oil to the lined baking sheet.

Pour enough oil into the pot to come about halfway up the sides. Heat over high heat until the oil is 350°F on a deep-frying thermometer. In batches and without crowding, carefully add the meatballs to the oil. Keeping the heat on high, fry the meatballs until they are golden brown, 2 to 3 minutes depending on the size of the balls. Use the spider to transfer the fried balls to the lined baking sheet. Keep warm in the oven while frying the remaining balls. Reheat the oil to 350°F between batches.

Grilling

Until a new utensil, the meatball grilling basket, came on the market, grilling was the least common method for making meatballs. The basket, which is hinged with a dozen indentations to hold and mold the balls into perfect orbs, is perforated or made of open mesh to allow the heat to penetrate. True meatball lovers will not want to be without one. You can still grill meatballs directly on the cooking grate, but they won't be as perfectly shaped.

For a charcoal grill, build a medium-hot fire. Let the coals burn until they are covered with white ash, then let them burn a few minutes longer, until you can hold your hand just above the cooking grate for 3 to 4 seconds. For a gas grill, preheat on high, then adjust the heat to medium-high (about 500°F).

To grill meatballs with a meatball basket, spray the inside of the basket with cooking spray or vegetable oil from a pump sprayer. Place the meatballs in the basket and close it. Put the basket on the grill and close the lid. Grill the meatballs, flipping the basket over halfway through, until the meatballs are nicely browned, 6 to 8 minutes depending on the desired doneness.

To grill the meatballs without a basket, scrub the cooking grate as clean as possible. Lightly oil the grate with a wad of paper towels dipped in vegetable oil, taking care not to let the oil drip and cause flare-ups. When shaping the meatballs, use oiled hands, as a light oil coating is added insurance against sticking. Place the shaped meatballs on the grill and cover. Grill until the undersides are lightly browned, about 3 minutes. Flip the meatballs and grill until the other sides are lightly browned and the meatballs are cooked through or to your desired doneness, about 3 to 5 minutes longer. Transfer to a platter.

Steaming

A method that yields especially moist and juicy meatballs, steaming is usually reserved for

Asian-style appetizers. You will need a stacked steamer set, available at Asian markets and grocers. Bamboo steamers may be the most familiar, but they have their issues, as they eventually absorb food flavors. A metal aluminum or stainless steel steamer is a better investment, as it is larger and deeper than a bamboo model, and easier to clean.

For either model, choose a saucepan just large enough to hold the stacked steamers. (Some metal steamers come with a bottom unit to replace the saucepan.) Pour about 1 inch of water into the saucepan and bring to a boil over high heat. Meanwhile, line the steamer trays with rounds of parchment paper or lettuce leaves to keep the meatballs from sticking to the steamer. Without crowding, place the meatballs in the lined trays. (In some recipes, the meatballs are placed in small bowls, and the bowls are placed in the steamer.) Stack the trays (smaller batches may only use one tray), place in the saucepan over the simmering water, and cover tightly with the steamer lid. Reduce the heat to medium-low to keep the water steaming at a robust simmer, and cook for the time indicated in the recipe. Meatballs cook in a relatively short period, so you probably won't have to worry about replacing the evaporated water, but check just to be sure. Remove the steamers from the saucepan, and transfer the meatballs to their serving dish.

Regardless of the cooking method—pan-cooking, baking, braising, deep-frying, grilling, or steaming—meatballs are as much fun to make as they are to eat. I love meatballs . . . and I know I am not alone!

CHOPPING YOUR OWN

Of course, every supermarket carries ground meat and poultry, and it is perfectly fine for everyday cooking. However, when I am serving meatballs to guests, I often chop my meat at home in my food processor. (Because I am not using a rotary meat grinder, I stop short of calling it ground meat.) The slightly coarse texture of the finished meatballs is noticeable as being prepared at home instead of industrially, and for very little effort, the dish's quality gets bumped up a notch.

Home-chopped meat has other advantages as well. First, you can trim the meat of excess fat (remember that fat provides flavor and moisture, so don't be too zealous). It also allows you to use organic or grass-fed meats. The texture of the chopped meat can be controlled to match your personal taste (I like a coarse chop). And, unfortunately, the practice of grinding meat fresh to order is long gone, except at the very best artisanal butchers.

Chopping is easily accomplished in a food processor and you don't need a separate rotary-blade meat grinder, although you can use one if you like. Some heavy-duty standing electric mixers have meat grinder attachments, but I find them bulky and difficult to clean, and I much prefer the food processor method.

To start, purchase naturally well-marbled cuts of meat that aren't excessively fatty. My preferred beef cuts for home-chopping are boneless flank and chuck. Supermarket ground round is my favorite ground beef for meatballs, but the round sold for stews and pot roasts is too lean for home-chopping. For other home-chopped meats, use shoulder or butt for pork, shoulder for lamb, and shoulder for veal. Because ground poultry should include skin, an ingredient that does not grind well at home, I stick to red meats and seafood for home-chopping.

Trim off most of the visible outer layer of fat from the meat. Cut the trimmed meat into 1- to 2-inch chunks and spread on a baking sheet. To make the meat easier to chop in the processor, freeze it until it is partially frozen and fairly firm, about 1 hour. In batches, add the partially frozen meat to the food processor fitted with the metal chopping blade. Pulse in 1- to 2-second bursts until the meat is chopped to your desired texture. I find that 10 pulses is usually sufficient. Transfer the chopped meat to a bowl.

When my buddy and meat expert Bruce Aidells and I were swapping recipes for this book, he told me that the best chopped meat he ever had was prepared by hand from a Chinese butcher who wielded two heavy cleavers. That may be true, but I have to draw the line somewhere.

meatballs
to start

spanish meatball tapas
with sherry-garlic sauce

spanish meatballs

12 ounces ground round
(85 percent lean)

12 ounces ground pork

¾ cup fresh bread crumbs

1 large egg, beaten

2 cloves garlic, minced

1 teaspoon sweet Spanish or
Hungarian paprika

1¾ teaspoons kosher salt

¼ teaspoon freshly ground
black pepper

2 tablespoons olive oil,
or more as needed

⅓ cup all-purpose flour

Albóndigas are almost always part of a tapas menu. While you may find them served in a red tomato or green herb sauce, it is this garlicky sherry sauce that really says "tapas" to me. Serve them communally, right from the skillet, as the residual heat helps keep them warm. Be sure to offer lots of crusty bread to wipe up every last drop of the sauce.

1. To make the meatballs, combine the ground round, ground pork, bread crumbs, egg, garlic, paprika, salt, and pepper in a large bowl and mix well. Cover and refrigerate for at least 15 minutes or up to 4 hours.

2. Using your wet hands rinsed under cold water, shape the mixture into 32 equal small meatballs. Transfer to a baking sheet.

3. Heat the oil in a large nonstick skillet over medium heat. In batches, roll the meatballs in the flour to coat, shaking off the excess flour. Add the meatballs to the skillet and cook, turning occasionally and adding more oil as needed, until lightly browned on all sides, about 5 minutes. Transfer to a plate.

4. To make the sauce, let the skillet cool for a few minutes. (If the garlic is added to a very hot skillet, it could easily burn and ruin the sauce.) Add the oil and garlic to the skillet. Stir over low heat until the garlic softens, about 1 minute. Add the sherry and increase the heat to high. Bring to a boil, scraping up the browned bits in the skillet with a wooden spoon. Stir in the broth. Return the meatballs

sherry-garlic sauce

1 tablespoon olive oil

4 cloves garlic, minced

½ cup dry sherry, such as La Ina (see Note)

¼ cup canned reduced-sodium chicken broth

Chopped fresh parsley, for garnish

Wooden toothpicks, for serving

to the skillet and reduce the heat to medium-low. Cover and simmer until the meatballs are cooked through and the sauce is lightly thickened, about 10 minutes. Season the sauce with salt and pepper.

5. Sprinkle the meatballs with parsley and serve, directly from the skillet, with toothpicks for spearing.

NOTE: There are many different kinds of sherry and some of them (such as cream or *amontillado*) are too sweet for general cooking. Look for brands that clearly identify themselves as dry (but not the brand Dry Sack, which is only medium-dry). La Ina is a reliable choice.

fried olive meatballs

makes 6 to 8 servings

olive meatballs

1 tablespoon olive oil

⅓ cup minced yellow onion

1 small clove garlic, minced

4 ounces ground pork

4 ounces ground round
(85 percent lean)

2 tablespoons dried plain
bread crumbs

1 tablespoon freshly grated
Parmesan cheese

1 large egg yolk

½ teaspoon dried oregano

½ teaspoon kosher salt

¼ teaspoon freshly
ground black pepper

24 pimento-stuffed olives

My first experience with fried meat-stuffed olives was in Tuscany, where they were served with pre-dinner glasses of Chianti. My first attempt at stuffing olives proved to be more frustrating than threading a needle without glasses. However, the reverse—stuffing meatballs with olives—was much easier, and just as tasty. These burst with flavor, so serve them with something equally hearty, such as . . . well, Chianti.

1. To make the meatballs, line a baking sheet with wax paper. Heat the oil in a small skillet over medium heat. Add the onion and cook until tender, about 3 minutes. Stir in the garlic and cook until fragrant, about 1 minute more. Transfer to a medium bowl and let cool.

2. Add the ground pork, ground round, bread crumbs, Parmesan, egg yolk, oregano, salt, and pepper to the onion and mix well. Using your wet hands rinsed under cold water, shape the meat mixture into 24 equal small balls. One at a time, flatten a ball slightly in your palms and completely wrap an olive with the meat mixture. Transfer to the wax paper–lined baking sheet.

3. To fry the meatballs, position a rack in the center of the oven and preheat to 200°F. Place a second baking sheet lined with a brown paper bag near the stove. Pour enough oil into a large saucepan to come halfway up the sides. Heat to 350°F on a deep-frying thermometer.

4. Spread the flour in a shallow bowl. Whisk the egg, salt, and pepper in another bowl. Combine the bread crumbs and oregano

Vegetable oil, for deep-frying

½ cup all-purpose flour

1 large egg, beaten

½ teaspoon kosher salt

¼ teaspoon freshly ground
black pepper

½ cup dried plain
bread crumbs

½ teaspoon dried oregano

Wooden toothpicks,
for serving

in a third shallow bowl. Roll each meatball in the flour, then dip in the egg, and then coat with the bread crumbs. Return to the wax paper–lined baking sheet.

5. In batches, deep-fry the meatballs in the hot oil until golden brown, about 2 minutes. Using a wire spider or slotted spoon, transfer the meatballs to the paper-lined baking sheet. Keep the meatballs warm in the oven while frying the remaining balls. Reheat the oil to 350°F between batches.

6. Transfer the meatballs to a platter and serve warm, with toothpicks for spearing.

braised vietnamese meatballs
in caramel sauce

vietnamese meatballs

3 tablespoons long-grain rice

1½ pounds ground pork

¼ cup finely chopped shallots

3 tablespoons Asian fish sauce (*nam pla* or *nuoc mam*)

2 tablespoons minced fresh cilantro

2 tablespoons minced fresh mint

1 clove garlic, minced

¼ teaspoon kosher salt

½ teaspoon freshly ground black pepper

savory vietnamese caramel sauce

¾ cup sugar

1 cup canned reduced-sodium chicken broth

3 tablespoons Asian fish sauce (*nam pla* or *nuoc mam*)

4 tablespoons vegetable oil

½ cup sliced shallots

2 tablespoons minced lemongrass (see page 107)

1 tablespoon peeled and minced fresh ginger

3 cloves garlic, minced

1 small Thai or serrano chile, cut crosswise into thin rounds

Fresh cilantro sprigs, for garnish

Wooden toothpicks, for serving

One could call this dish the basic Southeast Asian version of meatballs, but with such an explosion of flavors, and an unusual binder of ground toasted rice, there is nothing basic or commonplace about them. The salty-sweet-savory sauce makes them perfect for serving by themselves as an appetizer with drinks, or on a bowl of jasmine rice as a main course. You'll find a variation of these meatballs in the Vietnamese Banh Mi recipe on page 48.

1. To make the meatballs, heat an empty small skillet (not nonstick) over medium heat. Add the rice and cook, stirring often, until lightly toasted, about 3 minutes. Pour onto a plate and cool completely. Transfer to a coffee grinder and process until powdery.

2. Combine the ground rice, ground pork, shallots, fish sauce, cilantro, mint, garlic, salt, and pepper in a large bowl and mix well. Cover and refrigerate for at least 15 minutes or up to 4 hours.

3. Meanwhile, start the sauce. Combine the sugar and ¼ cup water in a medium saucepan. Bring to a boil over high heat, stirring constantly to dissolve the sugar. When the sugar dissolves, cook without stirring, occasionally swirling the saucepan by its handle to combine the syrup and washing down any crystals on the inside of the saucepan with a bristle pastry brush dipped in cold water, until the mixture is lightly smoking and caramelizes to the color of an old penny, about 4 minutes. Carefully add the broth and fish sauce (the mixture will splatter and harden), and stir until the caramel is dissolved. Remove from the heat.

4. Using your wet hands rinsed under cold water, shape the meat mixture into 16 equal meatballs. Heat 2 tablespoons of the oil in a large skillet over medium heat. In batches, add the meatballs and cook, turning occasionally, until lightly browned, about 5 minutes. Transfer to a plate.

5. Add the remaining 2 tablespoons oil to the skillet. Add the shallots, lemongrass, ginger, garlic, and chile. Cook over medium heat, stirring occasionally, until the shallots soften, about 2 minutes. Pour in the reserved caramel mixture and bring to a boil, stirring up any browned bits in the skillet with a wooden spatula. Return the meatballs to the skillet. Reduce the heat to medium-low and cover. Cook until the meatballs are cooked through and the sauce is lightly thickened, about 10 minutes. Garnish with the cilantro, and serve hot with small serving plates and forks.

vietnamese beef meatballs: Substitute 1½ pounds ground round for the ground pork.

fried thai pork and shrimp balls

8 ounces medium shrimp, peeled and deveined

1 pound ground pork

2 tablespoons Asian fish sauce (*nam pla* or *nuoc mam*)

1 scallion, white and green parts, finely chopped

1 tablespoon finely chopped fresh mint

1 tablespoon finely chopped fresh cilantro

1 tablespoon peeled and shredded fresh ginger (use the large holes on a box grater)

1 tablespoon cornstarch, plus more for dusting

1 small Thai or serrano chile, seeded and minced

1 teaspoon kosher salt

Vegetable oil, for deep-frying

Thai sweet chili garlic sauce, for serving

Wooden toothpicks, for serving

Southeast Asian food relies on the artful blend of herbs for its intriguing flavors, and these meatballs bring mint, cilantro, scallion, ginger, and chile into play. It's a good idea to keep a bottle of Thai sweet chili garlic sauce in the refrigerator, ready to use as a quick dip for Asian snacks like these tasty deep-fried nibbles. Buying it used to mean a trip to an Asian market, but now the sauce is carried at most supermarkets, as are fish sauce and other ingredients.

1. Process the shrimp in a food processor fitted with the chopping blade until very finely chopped into a paste. Add the ground pork and pulse until combined. Add the fish sauce, scallion, mint, cilantro, ginger, cornstarch, minced chile, and salt and pulse 5 or 6 times, just until combined. Transfer to a bowl and cover. Refrigerate for at least 15 minutes or up to 2 hours.

2. Line a rimmed baking sheet with wax paper and dust with cornstarch. Using your wet hands rinsed under cold water, shape the pork mixture into 36 equal small balls, placing the balls on the wax paper–lined baking sheet. Refrigerate for 15 minutes.

3. Position a rack in the center of the oven and preheat to 200°F. Place a wire cake rack on a second unlined baking sheet and put near the stove. Pour enough oil into a large, heavy saucepan to come about halfway up the sides. Heat over high heat to 350°F on a deep-frying thermometer. In batches, carefully add the balls to the oil one at a time and deep-fry until golden brown, about 2½ minutes. Using a wire spider, remove the balls from the oil and transfer to the wire rack. Keep warm in the oven while frying the remaining balls. Reheat the oil to 350°F between batches.

4. Pour the chili sauce into a serving bowl. Transfer the balls to a platter. Serve warm, with the sauce as a dip and toothpicks for spearing.

crunchy thai pork and shrimp balls:

Spread ½ cup cornstarch in a shallow bowl. Beat 2 large eggs together in a second shallow bowl. Spread 1½ cups panko in a third shallow bowl. Roll each ball in the cornstarch, then the eggs, then the panko. Place on a baking sheet and let stand for 10 minutes before deep-frying.

greek meatballs with tzatziki

makes **4** to **6** servings

tzatziki

2 standard cucumbers

1 teaspoon kosher salt

1 cup Greek-style yogurt
(see Note)

1 tablespoon fresh
lemon juice

1 tablespoon finely chopped
fresh mint

2 cloves garlic, crushed
though a press

¼ teaspoon freshly ground
black pepper

greek meatballs

1 cup fresh bread crumbs

½ cup milk

1½ pounds ground round
(85 percent lean), or use
half ground round and half
ground lamb

1 medium yellow onion,
shredded on the large holes
of a box grater

4 cloves garlic, crushed
through a press

2 large eggs, beaten

2 tablespoons chopped
fresh mint

2 teaspoons dried oregano

1½ teaspoons kosher salt

½ teaspoon freshly ground
black pepper

¼ teaspoon ground
cinnamon

3 tablespoons olive oil

Wooden toothpicks,
for serving

The first time I made these Greek-style meatballs, the unusual seasoning of fresh mint, dried oregano, and ground cinnamon had my guests asking for more. The cool yogurt-and-cucumber sauce is a great counterpoint. I prefer these with equal amounts of beef and lamb, but you can use either meat by itself. Great as pre-dinner nibbles, the *keftedes* are also good for dinner with buttered rice and a salad of cucumbers and tomatoes, or tuck them into a pita with shredded lettuce for a Greek-style sandwich.

1. To make the tzatziki, peel the cucumbers. Cut each in half lengthwise and scoop out the seeds with a spoon. Shred on the large holes of a box grater. Transfer to a wire sieve and toss with the salt. Let drain in the sink for 30 minutes to 1 hour. A handful at a time, squeeze the shredded cucumbers to extract more liquid, then transfer to a medium bowl. Add the yogurt, lemon juice, mint, garlic, and pepper

and mix well. Cover and refrigerate for at least 30 minutes or up to 2 days.

2. To make the meatballs, combine the bread crumbs and milk in a large bowl. Let stand until the bread crumbs are thoroughly moistened, about 3 minutes. Add the ground meat, onion, garlic, eggs, mint, oregano, salt, pepper, and cinnamon. Use your hands to mix the meat mixture well. Cover and refrigerate for at least 15 minutes or up to 4 hours.

3. Preheat the oven to 200°F. Using your wet hands rinsed under cold water, shape the meat mixture into 18 equal meatballs. Transfer the meatballs to a plate. Heat the oil in a large skillet (preferably nonstick) over medium heat. In batches, add the meatballs and cook, turning occasionally, until lightly browned and cooked through, 8 to 10 minutes. Transfer to a baking sheet and keep warm in the oven while cooking the remaining meatballs.

4. Spoon the tzatziki into individual ramekins or small serving bowls. Drain the meatballs briefly on paper towels. Serve the meatballs hot, with toothpicks for spearing and the tzatziki as a dip.

NOTE: Thick Greek-style yogurt is excellent, but not inexpensive. You can get similar results by draining regular yogurt. Line a wire sieve with rinsed, wrung-out cheesecloth and place in a large bowl, being sure that the bottom of the sieve is suspended at least an inch above the bottom of the bowl. Place 2 cups plain yogurt in the sieve and let stand for 1 to 2 hours to drain the excess whey and thicken the yogurt. You should have 1 cup drained yogurt.

chafing dish meatballs

makes **12** servings

meatballs

2 pounds ground round (85 percent lean)

¾ cup dried plain bread crumbs

2 large eggs, beaten

2 teaspoons kosher salt

½ teaspoon granulated garlic

½ teaspoon freshly ground black pepper

easy sweet-and-sour sauce

1 (12-ounce) bottle chili sauce

1 cup grape jelly

Wooden toothpicks, for serving

I am almost embarrassed to include this amazingly simple dish. I have made half-hearted attempts to remove it from my appetizer repertoire, but my friends' appeals keep it on the roster. So a chafing dish of meatballs is a standard at my holiday parties, where they disappear quickly. So, for your next bash, polish up your chafing dish and serve these gems, which have saved many a busy host.

1. To make the meatballs, combine the ground round, bread crumbs, eggs, salt, granulated garlic, and pepper and mix well. Cover and refrigerate for at least 15 minutes or up to 4 hours.

2. Position racks in the center and top third of the oven and preheat to 375°F. Lightly oil 2 rimmed baking sheets.

3. Using your wet hands rinsed under cold water, shape the meat mixture into 4 dozen equal small meatballs. Arrange on the baking sheets. Bake until lightly browned and cooked through, 20 to 25 minutes.

4. To make the sauce, bring the chili sauce and jelly to a boil in a Dutch oven or flameproof casserole over medium heat, stirring often. Add the meatballs and reduce the heat to medium-low. Simmer until the sauce thickens slightly, about 5 minutes. Transfer to a chafing dish or slow cooker to keep warm. Serve hot, with toothpicks for spearing.

maryland crab balls
with pink tartar sauce

makes 6 servings

pink tartar sauce

½ cup mayonnaise

2 tablespoons cocktail sauce

1½ tablespoons minced dill pickles or cornichons

1 tablespoon drained and rinsed nonpareil capers

1 scallion, white part only, minced

crab balls

1 pound crabmeat, picked over for shells and cartilage

⅓ cup plus ½ cup cracker meal or dried plain bread crumbs

¼ cup mayonnaise

1 large egg yolk

2 teaspoons Worcestershire sauce

1 teaspoon Old Bay Seasoning

½ teaspoon hot red pepper sauce

Vegetable oil, for deep-frying

Wooden toothpicks, for serving

In the Chesapeake Bay region, not far from where I live, crab is king. While the crustacean is turned into a number of tasty appetizers, including dips and spreads, it reaches its epitome in these crispy balls. Great at backyard parties with cold beer, they also make fine sandwiches (see variation below). For the true Baltimore flavor, use Old Bay Seasoning, which can be found at every supermarket.

1. To make the tartar sauce, combine the mayonnaise, cocktail sauce, pickles, capers, and scallion in a small bowl and mix well. Cover and refrigerate until serving.

2. To make the crab balls, combine the crabmeat, ⅓ cup of the cracker meal, the mayonnaise, egg yolk, Worcestershire sauce, Old Bay, and hot pepper sauce in a medium bowl and mix well. Cover and refrigerate for at least 15 minutes or up to 4 hours.

3. Position a rack in the center of the oven and preheat to 200°F. Place a wire cake rack on an unlined baking sheet and put near the stove.

4. Spread the remaining ½ cup cracker meal in a shallow bowl. Line a second baking sheet with wax paper. Using your wet hands rinsed under cold water, shape the crabmeat mixture into 18 equal balls. Roll each in the cracker meal to coat and place on the wax paper–lined baking sheet.

5. Pour enough oil into a large, heavy saucepan to come about halfway up the sides. Heat over high heat to 350°F on a deep-frying thermometer. In batches, carefully add the balls to the oil one at a time and deep-fry until golden brown, about 2½ minutes. Using a wire spider, remove the balls from the oil and transfer to the wire rack. Keep warm in the oven while frying the remaining balls. Reheat the oil to 350°F between batches.

6. Serve the crab balls warm, with the sauce as a dip and toothpicks for spearing.

crab ball sandwiches: Split 6 soft oblong rolls. Spread with Pink Tartar Sauce. Add 3 crab balls to each, and top with shredded iceberg lettuce and tomato slices. Makes 6 servings.

chinese rice-crusted meatballs
with soy-ginger dip

chinese meatballs

⅔ cup long-grain rice

4 ounces medium shrimp, peeled and deveined

12 ounces ground pork

4 canned water chestnuts, drained and minced

1 scallion, white and pale green parts only (reserve dark green top for garnish), minced

1 tablespoon soy sauce

1 tablespoon Chinese rice wine or dry sherry

2 teaspoons peeled and minced fresh ginger

1 teaspoon Asian dark sesame oil

½ teaspoon sugar

½ teaspoon kosher salt

¼ teaspoon freshly ground black pepper

soy-ginger dipping sauce

¼ cup soy sauce

2 quarter-sized slices peeled fresh ginger, cut into thin strips

Wooden toothpicks, for serving

1 scallion, dark green top only, minced, for garnish

When the cocktail theme is Asian, serve these Chinese-style meatballs—they are excellent with chilled sake. Steaming imparts a delicate texture, and a rice coating gives the balls a mottled appearance. The rice must be soaked for 3 hours before cooking, so be sure to allow this extra time. You will need stacked bamboo or metal steamers, available at Asian grocers and some kitchenware stores. The steamers must be lined with parchment paper before adding the meatballs to avoid sticking. If you don't have parchment, use large lettuce leaves, as the coating on wax paper could melt from the hot steam.

1. To make the meatballs, place the rice in a medium bowl and add enough cold water to cover by 1 inch. Let stand for 3 hours.

2. Pulse the shrimp in a food processor fitted with the chopping blade until very finely chopped into a paste. Add the ground pork and pulse until combined. Transfer to a medium bowl. Add the water chestnuts, white and pale green parts of the scallion, soy sauce, rice wine, ginger, sesame oil, sugar, salt, and pepper and mix well. Cover and refrigerate for at least 15 minutes or up to 2 hours.

3. Line 2 bamboo or metal steamer racks with parchment paper. Pour about 2 inches of water into a large saucepan that will comfortably support the steamers and bring to a boil over high heat. (If using a metal steamer set, add 1 inch of water to the bottom section and bring to a boil.) Reduce the heat to medium-low to maintain a full head of steam.

4. Drain the rice well in a wire sieve. Return the soaked rice to the bowl. Using your wet hands rinsed under cold water, shape the pork mixture into 24 equal balls. Roll each ball in the rice to coat. Arrange the balls, 1 inch apart, in the steamers.

5. Stack the steamers over the saucepan and cover. Steam until the rice is tender and the balls are cooked through, about 20 minutes.

6. Meanwhile, to make the dipping sauce, combine the soy sauce and ginger in a small serving bowl.

7. Transfer the balls to a platter and stick a toothpick into each. Sprinkle with the minced scallion top. Serve hot with the dipping sauce.

USING STORE-BOUGHT MEATBALLS

When you want meatballs but don't have the time to make them from scratch, there is a solution. Just make one of the sauces below, and add store-bought meatballs. There are many brands available, usually made from beef. You are sure to find frozen meatballs in 5-pound bags at wholesale clubs like Costco, or in smaller amounts at your supermarket, where they might be in the refrigerated prepared meat section. Simply add the meatballs to the sauce and simmer until they are heated through, about 15 minutes (cook a few minutes longer for frozen meatballs). Of course, if you would like to use homemade frozen meatballs, there is a list of versatile recipes appropriate for freezing on page 77.

Here are the sauces in the book that work well with store-bought (or frozen homemade) meatballs:

Amatriciana Sauce (page 138)
Beefy Pasta Sauce (page 123)
Bolognese Sauce (page 133)
Bourguignon Sauce (page 65)
Caper Sauce (page 71)
Chile Verde (page 72)
Classic Tomato Pasta Sauce (page 124)
Easy Brown Sauce (page 74)
Easy Sweet-and-Sour Sauce (page 13)
Everyday Tomato Sauce (page 127)
Fresh Basil and Tomato Sauce (page 136)
Green Curry Sauce (page 90)
Horseradish Sauce (page 88)
Marsala-Mushroom Sauce (page 131)
Savory Vietnamese Caramel Sauce
  (page 6)
Spinach-Coriander Sauce (page 93)

beef dim sum
with mustard greens

4 ounces sliced fresh pork fatback (see Note)

1 pound ground round (85 percent lean)

1 scallion, white and green parts, minced

1 tablespoon peeled and minced fresh ginger

3 cloves garlic, minced

1 large egg, beaten

2 tablespoons dark soy sauce, or 2 tablespoons regular soy sauce plus 1 teaspoon molasses, plus more for serving

1 tablespoon dry sherry

1 tablespoon cornstarch

1 teaspoon Asian dark sesame oil

1 teaspoon kosher salt

¼ teaspoon freshly ground black pepper

12 stems mustard greens or broccoli rabe (rapini), washed well

Steaming yields the moistest, juiciest meatballs of all. At a dim sum restaurant, it is difficult to resist beef meatballs, often cooked with a few leaves of verdant bitter greens as a bracing contrast. The meatballs and greens are steamed together in small dishes to mingle their juices, requiring a set of tiered metal or bamboo steaming racks. An Asian market will have the proper traditional porcelain bowls (about 3 inches wide and 1 inch deep), or simply use large ramekins or Pyrex custard cups.

1. Coarsely chop the sliced fatback. Spread on a baking sheet and freeze until semisolid, about 45 minutes. (This makes the fat easier to chop in the food processor.)

2. Transfer the fatback to a food processor fitted with the metal chopping blade. Pulse about 10 times, until finely chopped. Add the ground round, scallion, ginger, garlic, egg, soy sauce, sherry, cornstarch, sesame oil, salt, and pepper. Pulse about 6 more times, until the mixture is well combined. Transfer to a medium bowl. Cover and refrigerate for at least 15 minutes or up to 4 hours. Using your hands rinsed under cold water, shape into 18 equal meatballs. Transfer to a platter.

3. Have ready 6 small Asian heatproof dim sum dishes, 8-ounce ramekins, or 10-ounce Pryex custard cups. Tear 2 mustard greens crosswise and fit into each dish. Add 3 meatballs to each dish.

4. Choose a saucepan just large enough to hold the stacked steamers. Pour about 1 inch of water into the saucepan and bring to a boil over high heat. (If using a metal steamer set, add 1 inch of water to the bottom section and bring to a boil.) Arrange the filled dishes in 2 steamer racks. Stack over the saucepan and cover with the steamer lid. Reduce the heat to medium-low to maintain a full head of steam. Cook until the meatballs are cooked through, about 15 minutes.

5. Using tongs (preferably rubber tipped, which have the best grip), carefully remove the dishes from the steamers. Serve hot, with dark or regular soy sauce passed on the side.

NOTE: Fresh pork fatback, pure white fat cut from pork loin, is available at Asian and Latino markets. Do not confuse it with salt pork. If unavailable, substitute ground pork, which does not need to be frozen or chopped before using. For the correct smooth texture, pulse all of the ingredients in a food processor until well combined and very finely chopped.

meatballs
in your soup

mexican chipotle
albóndigas soup

meatballs

1 pound ground round
(85 percent lean)

1 medium yellow onion,
shredded on the large holes
of a box grater

2 cloves garlic, crushed
through a press

3 tablespoons yellow
cornmeal, preferably
stone-ground

1 large egg, beaten

2 teaspoons adobo sauce
from canned chipotle chiles

1 teaspoon dried oregano

1 teaspoon kosher salt

½ cup long-grain rice

soup

2 tablespoons olive oil

1 large yellow onion, chopped

2 cloves garlic, minced

1 teaspoon dried oregano

1 teaspoon ground cumin

5 cups canned reduced-
sodium chicken broth

1 (28-ounce) can plum
tomatoes in juice, chopped,
juices reserved

2 medium zucchini, trimmed
and cut into ½-inch dice

1 chipotle chile, minced
(see box)

2 cups fresh or thawed
frozen corn kernels

Kosher salt and freshly
ground black pepper

Mexican *crema* or sour
cream, for serving

I spent my first college semester in Guadalajara, where I learned the rudiments of the local cuisine from my host family. The lady of the house, Señora Macías, often served her houseful of hungry American students this hearty soup/stew. It is loaded with Mexican meatballs (*albóndigas*), which are made with rice to stretch a pound of beef. My current version gets a little more zing from smoky chipotles.

1. To make the meatballs, mix the ground round, onion, garlic, cornmeal, egg, adobo sauce, oregano, and salt in a large bowl until barely combined. Add the rice and mix until thoroughly combined. Cover and refrigerate for at least 15 minutes or up to 2 hours.

2. To make the soup, heat the oil in a Dutch oven or large saucepan over medium heat. Add the onion and cook, stirring occasionally, until softened, about 5 minutes.

Stir in the garlic, oregano, and cumin and cook until fragrant, about 1 minute. Add the broth, tomatoes with their juices, zucchini, and chipotle and bring to a boil over high heat. Return the heat to medium to keep at a steady simmer.

3. Using your wet hands rinsed under cold water, shape the meat mixture into 24 equal meatballs. Transfer to a platter. One at a time, drop the meatballs into the Dutch oven—they will firm up when they hit the simmering broth. Cover with the lid ajar and simmer until the rice is tender, about 25 minutes. During the last 5 minutes, add the corn. Season with salt and pepper. Serve hot, topping each serving with a dollop of *crema*.

CHIPOTLES

Chipotle chile peppers, which are smoked jalapeños, are most commonly available in small cans, packed with a thick spicy chile sauce called adobo. (Chipotle is also available as a pure ground powder and whole dried peppers, neither of which includes adobo sauce.) The chiles are extremely spicy, so if you have sensitive skin, wear plastic gloves—at least, use an extra measure of caution when handling them. There are six or seven chiles in each can, so leftovers are likely. After opening the can, transfer the remaining chiles and adobo to a small covered container (use an inexpensive disposable one, such as a plastic 1-cup delicatessen take-out container or a recycled jar, as the red adobo will stain and transfer its flavor). Refrigerated, the chiles will keep for a month or two. Freeze for longer storage: Line a baking sheet with parchment or wax paper. Place the chiles about 1 inch apart on the baking sheet. Spoon equal amounts of the adobo in the can over each chile. Freeze until the chiles and sauce are solid and can be lifted from the paper. Transfer to a zip-top plastic storage bag and freeze for up to 6 months. They can now be used as needed, one at a time, with the adobo clinging to the chile.

pho with beef meatballs

spiced beef broth

1½ pounds beef marrow bones

1½ pounds meaty beef bones, such as beef barbecue ribs, shank, or short ribs

1 medium yellow onion, sliced

1 (3-inch) cinnamon stick

8 quarter-sized slices unpeeled fresh ginger

2 teaspoons coriander seeds

1 teaspoon black peppercorns

3 star anise

4 whole cloves

Asian fish sauce (*nam pla* or *nuoc mam*)

Kosher salt

meatballs

1 pound ground round (85 percent lean)

1 tablespoon Asian fish sauce (*nam pla* or *nuoc mam*)

1 tablespoon cornstarch

1 teaspoon sugar

2 cloves garlic, minced

½ teaspoon baking powder

½ teaspoon freshly ground black pepper

noodles and condiments

1 pound (¼-inch-wide) rice noodles

1 cup fresh mint leaves

1 cup fresh Thai basil leaves

1 cup fresh cilantro leaves

2 medium carrots, cut into thin julienne

2 small red chiles, cut into thin rounds

2 limes, cut into 6 wedges each

Sriracha or other hot red pepper sauce

Hoisin sauce

Reflect on the past couple of decades of American cooking and you might be surprised at the amount of strictly ethnic dishes that have entered the mainstream. *Pho* (pronounced "fuh"), the Vietnamese noodle soup, is in this ever-growing group. Of course, the version with firm, almost chewy, meatballs is my favorite. The soup base must be made from scratch and not from doctored-up canned broth, but it requires little attention.

1. To make the broth, combine the marrow bones and meaty beef bones in a large pot and add enough cold water to cover by 1 inch, about 2¼ quarts. Bring to a boil over high heat, skimming off any foam that rises to the top. Add the sliced onion, cinnamon stick, ginger, coriander seeds, peppercorns, star anise, cloves, 1 tablespoon fish sauce, and 1 teaspoon kosher salt. Reduce the heat to low. Simmer until the broth is full-flavored, about 3 hours.

Strain through a large wire sieve set over a large heatproof bowl, discarding the solids. Return the broth to the pot and bring to a simmer over medium heat.

2. Meanwhile, make the meatballs. Mix the ground round, fish sauce, cornstarch, sugar, garlic, baking powder, and pepper together in a medium bowl. Cover and refrigerate for at least 15 minutes or up to 4 hours. Using your wet hands rinsed under cold water, shape the mixture into 18 equal meatballs. Transfer to a plate.

3. One at a time, drop the meatballs into the simmering broth. They will firm up when they hit the broth. Cover with the lid ajar and cook until the meatballs are cooked through, about 20 minutes.

4. While the meatballs are simmering, soak the rice noodles. Put in a large bowl and add enough hot tap water to cover by 1 inch. Let stand until softened and supple, about 10 minutes. Drain well and add to the broth. Season the broth with additional fish sauce and salt.

5. To serve, divide the mint, basil, cilantro, carrots, chiles, and lime wedges among 6 small bowls. Ladle the soup into 6 large bowls. Serve hot with the bowls of condiments, and the hot sauce and hoisin sauce passed on the side, allowing each guest to season the *pho* as they wish.

indonesian meatball soup

beef stock

2 tablespoons vegetable oil

1½ pounds meaty beef bones, such as beef barbecue ribs, shank, or short ribs

1½ pounds beef marrow bones

12 large cloves garlic, crushed under a knife and peeled

1 teaspoon black peppercorns

About 2 tablespoons soy sauce, as needed

meatballs

3 ice cubes

1½ pounds ground round (85 percent lean)

2 tablespoons cornstarch

1 large egg white

3 cloves garlic, crushed through a press

1¾ teaspoons kosher salt

½ teaspoon freshly ground black pepper

½ cup vegetable oil

6 square wonton noodles

6 baby bok choy

8 ounces thin Chinese-style lo mein noodles or egg noodles

Kecap manis and *sambal oelek* (see Note), for serving

This meal-in-a-bowl first came to the attention of most Americans when President Obama mentioned it as one of his favorite foods from his childhood in Indonesia. *Bakso*, a beloved soup often served by street vendors, starts with beef stock, meatballs, and noodles . . . and from there, it's up to the cook. I've used the most popular ingredients, but you could swap spinach for the baby bok choy, or substitute store-bought crispy noodles for the freshly fried wonton noodles. And in place of the lo mein noodles, you could use just about any kind of Asian noodle (soaked and drained rice and bean thread noodles, prepared as for the *pho* on page 27, are good). The Indonesian condiments *kecap manis* and *sambal oelek* supply the sweet-spicy-salty flavor that sets *bakso* apart from other Asian meatball soups.

1. To make the stock, heat the oil in a large pot over medium-high heat. Add the meaty beef bones and cook, turning occasionally, until browned, about 10 minutes. Add the marrow bones, garlic, and peppercorns. Pour in enough cold water to cover by 1 inch, about 2½ quarts. Bring to a boil over high heat, skimming off any foam that rises to the top. Reduce the heat to low. Simmer until the stock is full-flavored, about 3 hours. Strain through a large wire sieve set over a large heatproof bowl, discarding the solids. Let stand for 5 minutes, then skim any fat from the surface. Return the stock to the pot and return to a simmer over medium heat. Season with the soy sauce.

2. Meanwhile, to make the meatballs, fit a food processor with the metal chopping blade. With the machine running, drop the ice cubes through the feed tube to chop the ice. Stop the machine and add the ground round, cornstarch, egg white, garlic, salt, and pepper. Process until the mixture is smooth, about 20 seconds. (The ice cubes help firm the fat in the ground round and add moisture to the meatballs.)Transfer to a bowl and cover.

Refrigerate for at least 15 minutes or up to 4 hours.

3. To fry the wonton noodles, heat the vegetable oil in a medium skillet over high heat until shimmering. One at a time, add the wonton squares and fry, turning once, just until golden, 20 to 30 seconds. Transfer to paper towels to drain.

4. When ready to cook, using your wet hands rinsed under cold water, shape the meat mixture into 24 equal meatballs. Transfer the meatballs to a plate. One at a time, drop the meatballs into the simmering stock. They will firm up when they hit the stock. Cover with the lid ajar and cook until the meatballs are cooked through, about 20 minutes.

5. While the meatballs are cooking, bring a medium saucepan of lightly salted water to a boil over high heat. Add the baby bok choy and cook just until barely tender when pierced with the tip of a sharp knife, about 6 minutes. Drain and rinse under cold running water. Squeeze each bok choy gently to extract the excess water. Cut each in half lengthwise.

6. Bring a large saucepan of lightly salted water to a boil over high heat. Add the lo mein noodles and cook according to the package directions until tender. Drain and rinse under cold running water.

7. When the meatballs are done, add the bok choy and lo mein noodles to the stock and cook until heated through, about 2 minutes. Using tongs, transfer equal amounts of the noodles to 6 deep soup bowls, then add 2 bok choy halves. Divide the soup and meatballs evenly among the bowls. Top each with a fried wonton noodle. Serve hot. Pass the *kecap manis* and *sambal oelek* at the table for seasoning, which should be fairly generous— the soup should be spicy, salty, and sweet, all at once.

NOTE: *Kecap manis* (sweet, thick soy sauce) and *sambal oelek* (chili paste) are available at Asian grocers. If you can't find *kecap manis,* substitute ½ cup soy sauce whisked with ¼ cup molasses. Any Asian hot chili paste can stand in for the *sambal oelek.*

alphabet meatball soup

meatballs

1 pound ground round (85 percent lean)

⅓ cup dried plain bread crumbs

1 small yellow onion, shredded on the large holes of a box grater

1 large egg, beaten

1 tablespoon chopped fresh parsley

1¼ teaspoons kosher salt

¼ teaspoon freshly ground black pepper

soup

2 tablespoons vegetable oil

2 large leeks, white and pale green parts only, chopped, rinsed, and drained (2 cups)

2 medium carrots, cut into ½-inch dice

2 celery ribs, cut into ½-inch dice

3½ cups homemade beef stock or canned reduced-sodium beef broth

3 ripe plum tomatoes, seeded and chopped, or 1 cup drained and chopped canned tomatoes

2 tablespoons chopped fresh parsley

¼ teaspoon dried thyme

1 bay leaf

1 teaspoon kosher salt

¼ teaspoon freshly ground black pepper

⅓ cup alphabet noodles

Beef and vegetable soup is an old-fashioned dish I love that deserves to be made more often. Add alphabet noodles, and I am transported back to an earlier time in my life, sitting at my family's Formica table, eating lunch on a chilly day. Meatballs increase the nostalgic appeal of the timeless soup.

1. To make the meatballs, combine the ground round, bread crumbs, onion, egg, parsley, salt, and pepper in a medium bowl and mix well. Cover and refrigerate for at least 15 minutes or up to 4 hours. Using your hands rinsed under cold water, shape the mixture into 24 equal small meatballs. Transfer to a plate. Refrigerate while making the soup.

2. To make the soup, heat the oil in a large pot over medium heat. Add the leeks, carrots, and celery and cover. Cook, stirring occasionally, until the onion is softened, about 5 minutes. Stir in 4 cups water, the beef stock, tomatoes, parsley, thyme, bay leaf, salt, and pepper. Bring to a boil. Reduce the heat to medium-low and simmer, uncovered, for 10 minutes.

3. One at a time, add the meatballs to the soup. Cook until the meatballs are firm, about 20 minutes. Stir in the alphabet noodles and cook until tender, about 10 minutes.

4. Remove the bay leaf. Ladle the soup into bowls and serve hot.

chicken-matzo balls
in vegetable soup

chicken-matzo balls

1 pound ground chicken

⅓ cup matzo meal or dried plain bread crumbs

1 small onion, shredded on the large holes of a box grater

1 large egg, beaten

2 tablespoons chopped fresh parsley

1 teaspoon kosher salt

¼ teaspoon dried thyme

¼ teaspoon freshly ground black pepper

soup

2 tablespoons vegetable oil

1 medium yellow onion, chopped

2 medium celery ribs with leaves, ribs cut into ½-inch dice, leaves chopped

1 medium carrot, cut into ½-inch dice

6 cups canned reduced-sodium chicken broth

½ teaspoon dried thyme

1 bay leaf

Kosher salt and freshly ground black pepper

Chopped fresh parsley, for garnish

Chicken soup is renowned for its restorative qualities, but a really good one, made from a tough old chicken, takes a serious amount of simmering. However, ground chicken and fresh vegetables lend their flavors to canned chicken broth to make a satisfying soup in record time.

1. To make the chicken-matzo balls, mix the ground chicken, matzo meal, onion, egg, parsley, salt, thyme, and pepper together in a large bowl. Cover and refrigerate for at least 15 minutes or up to 4 hours.

2. To make the soup, heat the oil in a large pot over medium heat. Add the onion, celery, celery leaves, and carrot and cover. Cook, stirring occasionally, until the vegetables soften, about 5 minutes. Add the broth, thyme, and bay leaf and bring to a boil over high heat. Reduce the heat to medium-low, cover with the lid ajar, and simmer for 15 minutes.

3. Using your wet hands rinsed under cold water, shape the chicken mixture into 24 equal balls. Transfer to a platter. One at a time, drop the balls into the simmering soup. Simmer, with the lid ajar, until the meatballs are cooked through, about 20 minutes. Season with salt and pepper.

4. Discard the bay leaf. Ladle the soup into soup bowls, sprinkle with parsley, and serve hot.

meatball chili soup

chili meatballs

12 ounces ground round
(85 percent lean)

12 ounces ground pork

¾ cup cracker meal, crushed
saltine crackers, or dried
plain bread crumbs

1 medium yellow onion,
shredded on the large holes
of a box grater

2 cloves garlic, minced

2 large eggs, beaten

2 teaspoons chili powder

1¾ teaspoons kosher salt

The Texas legislature named chili as its state dish in 1977, but that hardly means that there is agreement on how the dish should be prepared. Arguments can quickly arise over the use of stewing meat, ground beef, tomatoes, beans, chili powder, or whole dried chiles. One thing for sure: Meatball chili is a very viable, and fun, alternative to the stewing meat version. Try it served over macaroni with a heap of shredded Cheddar cheese on top.

1. Position a rack in the center of the oven and preheat to 375°F. Lightly oil a large rimmed baking sheet.

2. To make the meatballs, combine the ground round, ground pork, cracker meal, onion, garlic, eggs, chili powder, and salt in a large bowl and mix well. Cover and refrigerate for at least 15 minutes or up to 4 hours. Using your wet hands rinsed under cold water, shape the meat mixture into 18 equal meatballs. Put the meatballs on the baking sheet. Bake until lightly browned, 20 to 25 minutes.

3. Meanwhile, make the soup. Heat the oil in a large Dutch oven or saucepan over medium heat. Add the onion, red and green peppers, and jalapeño and cook, stirring occasionally, until softened, about 10 minutes. Stir in the garlic and cook until fragrant, about 1 minute. Add the chili powder and stir for 30 seconds. Add the tomatoes with their puree and the broth, stir well, and bring to a boil. Reduce the heat to medium-low and simmer for 30 minutes.

chili soup

2 tablespoons olive oil

1 medium yellow onion, chopped

1 medium red bell pepper, seeded and chopped

1 medium green bell pepper, seeded and chopped

1 jalapeño, seeded and minced

2 cloves garlic, minced

2 tablespoons chili powder

1 (28-ounce) can plum tomatoes in puree, chopped

2 cups homemade beef stock or canned reduced-sodium beef broth

Kosher salt

1 (19-ounce) can pinto beans, drained and rinsed (optional)

4. Transfer the meatballs to the soup. Pour off and discard the fat from the baking sheet. Add 1 cup of the soup to the baking sheet, scrape up the browned bits with a wooden spatula, then pour back into the pot. Return the soup to a simmer and cook until reduced slightly, about 20 minutes. Season with salt. During the last 10 minutes, stir in the beans. Serve hot.

chinese shrimp ball soup

makes **4** to **6** servings

shrimp balls

1 pound large easy-peel shrimp

⅓ cup finely chopped carrot

1 scallion, minced

1 large egg, beaten

1 tablespoon cornstarch

2 teaspoons peeled and minced fresh ginger

½ teaspoon kosher salt

¼ teaspoon freshly ground white pepper

soup

Shrimp shells from the peeled shrimp

6 cups canned reduced-sodium chicken broth

2 tablespoons Chinese rice wine or dry sherry

3 scallions

4 quarter-sized slices unpeeled fresh ginger

2 cloves garlic

1 skein bean threads (*saifun*)

Soy sauce, for serving

Asian dark sesame oil, for serving

A classic of Chinese cooking, make this when you want meatballs on the light side. It lends itself to many additions—snow peas, baby spinach, watercress, and just about any other fresh green vegetable. Use ready-to-peel shrimp, and the soup comes together in no time. Be sure to save the shrimp shells to make the especially flavorful stock.

1. To make the shrimp balls, peel and devein the shrimp, reserving the shells for the soup. Pulse the shrimp meat in a food processor fitted with the chopping blade about 10 times, or until processed into a very coarse puree. Transfer to a bowl. Add the carrot, minced scallion, egg, cornstarch, ginger, salt, and pepper and mix well. Cover and refrigerate for at least 15 minutes or up to 2 hours.

2. To make the soup, combine the shrimp shells, broth, and rice wine in a pot. Crush 1 of the scallions, the ginger, and garlic under the flat side of a large knife and add to the pot. Bring to a boil over high heat. Reduce the heat to medium-low and simmer for 15 minutes to blend the flavors.

3. Meanwhile, put the bean threads in a medium bowl and add enough very hot tap water to cover. Let stand until the bean threads are pliable, about 10 minutes. Drain in a wire sieve and return to the bowl. Using kitchen scissors, snip through the threads to cut them into manageable lengths. Set aside.

4. Use a wire strainer to remove the solid ingredients from the soup and discard. Using a heaping tablespoon for each, drop spoonfuls of the shrimp mixture into the simmering broth—they

will firm up when they hit the broth. Do not attempt to shape the mixture into smooth balls with your hands. Cover and simmer until the shrimp balls are firm and cooked through, about 10 minutes.

5. Cut the white and green parts of the remaining 2 scallions into long, thin shreds about 2 inches long. Add the scallions and bean threads to the pot and cook just until heated through, about 1 minute more. Ladle into bowls and serve with soy sauce and sesame oil passed on the side for seasoning.

GRADING MEAT

The USDA has a voluntary meat-grading program, and understanding how it works helps the consumer make smart purchases. As a rule of thumb, a high meat grade indicates excellent flavor and tenderness. Beef, veal, and lamb are graded, but pork is considered to be so standardized that grading isn't called for. Poultry is inspected and graded, but Grade A is the only designation you are likely to see. The USDA does not have a grading system for seafood, and only imported seafood is inspected.

Prime, Choice, and Standard are the top three USDA meat inspection grades, and the ones sold to consumers at the retail level. Prime meat is especially tasty and tender, but there is no need to buy it for meatballs, because ground meat is constituted of tough cuts like round and chuck, and tenderness isn't a factor. (Besides, less than 3 percent of meat is graded Prime, and most of that goes to restaurants.) Choice, sold at many supermarkets and price clubs, is the grade I buy for my own use. Standard meat is only acceptable, and it is often the grade being sold when the price is too cheap to seem true.

escarole and
meatball soup

soup

1 tablespoon olive oil

1 large yellow onion, chopped

2 medium carrots, cut into ½-inch dice

2 medium celery ribs, cut into ½-inch dice

2 cloves garlic, minced

1 pound escarole, coarsely chopped

2 quarts canned reduced-sodium chicken broth

½ cup orzo

This beautifully seasoned soup, a staple of Italian-American cooking, is often called Wedding Soup, but it is not a dish that is traditionally served at Italian weddings. The connubial name refers to the marriage of meat and greens, or the fact that the original recipe included pairs of ingredients (two each onions, carrots, celery ribs, and the like). Be sure to rinse the escarole well, as it loves to hide grit in its curly nooks.

1. To make the soup, heat the oil in a large pot over medium heat. Add the onion, carrots, celery, and garlic and cover. Cook, stirring occasionally, until softened, about 5 minutes.

2. Meanwhile, place the escarole in a large bowl of cold water. Agitate the escarole in the water to loosen any grit, then let it stand for a minute so the grit sinks to the bottom of the bowl. Lift the escarole out of the water and transfer to another bowl. Repeat with fresh water. Shake the excess water off the escarole, but do not dry.

3. Add the escarole to the pot and stir well. Cover and cook until wilted, about 5 minutes. Pour in the broth and bring to a boil over high heat. Reduce the heat to medium-low and simmer, with the lid ajar, for 45 minutes.

meatballs

8 ounces ground round

8 ounces ground pork

½ cup dried Italian-seasoned bread crumbs

¼ cup freshly grated Parmesan cheese, plus more for serving

¼ cup whole milk

1 large egg, beaten

2 cloves garlic, crushed through a press

Kosher salt and freshly ground black pepper

4. Meanwhile, make the meatballs. Combine the ground round, ground pork, bread crumbs, Parmesan, milk, egg, garlic, 1 teaspoon salt, and ½ teaspoon pepper together in a medium bowl. Using your wet hands rinsed under cold water, shape into 60 equal small meatballs. Transfer to a baking sheet.

5. One at a time, drop the meatballs into the soup. They will firm up when they hit the broth. Add the orzo. Return the soup to a simmer over high heat, then reduce the heat to medium-low and cover with the lid ajar. Simmer until the meatballs are cooked through, about 15 minutes. Season the soup with salt and pepper. Serve hot, with Parmesan cheese passed on the side.

meatballs
between bread

turkey meatball subs
with cranberry-chipotle mayonnaise

makes **4** sandwiches

cranberry-chipotle mayonnaise

⅓ cup plus 1 tablespoon canned jellied cranberry sauce

¼ cup mayonnaise

1 teaspoon adobo sauce from canned chipotle chiles (see page 25)

turkey and sage meatballs

1¼ pounds ground turkey

½ cup dried plain bread crumbs

2 scallions, finely chopped

1 large egg plus 1 large egg white, beaten

1¼ teaspoons kosher salt

½ teaspoon dried sage

¼ teaspoon freshly ground black pepper

This recipe condenses many of the flavors of Thanksgiving dinner into a hearty sandwich, with an unexpected twist of smoky spiciness provided by chipotle adobo sauce. Use regular ground turkey with about 7 percent fat content, as the very lean ground turkey breast makes dry meatballs. These sandwiches don't have to be served piping hot—they are equally tasty at room temperature.

1. To make the mayonnaise, mix the cranberry sauce, mayonnaise, and adobo in a small bowl. Cover and refrigerate until ready to serve.

2. To make the meatballs, mix the turkey, bread crumbs, scallions, egg and egg white, salt, sage, and pepper together in a large bowl. Cover and refrigerate for at least 15 minutes or up to 4 hours.

3. Position oven racks in the center and top third of the oven and preheat to 375°F. Lightly oil a large rimmed baking sheet. Place the rolls, cut side up, on a second baking sheet (no need to grease this sheet).

4 whole-wheat submarine rolls, split lengthwise

4 green-leaf lettuce leaves, for serving

4. Using your wet hands rinsed under cold water, shape the turkey mixture into 16 equal meatballs. Place on the oiled baking sheet. Bake on the center rack for 20 minutes. Place the baking sheet with the rolls on the top rack and continue baking until the meatballs are lightly browned and cooked through and the rolls are heated, about 5 minutes more.

5. For each sandwich, spread about 2½ tablespoons of the cranberry-chipotle mayonnaise inside a roll, then add 4 meatballs and a lettuce leaf. Close the roll and serve.

vietnamese banh mi with quick pickled vegetables

quick pickled vegetables

⅓ cup unseasoned rice vinegar (not sushi vinegar)

1 tablespoon sugar

2 teaspoons kosher salt

2 medium carrots, cut into julienne

½ small daikon radish, cut into julienne

meatballs and caramel sauce

1¼ pounds ground pork

2 tablespoons minced shallots

2 tablespoons Asian fish sauce (*nam pla* or *nuoc mam*)

1 tablespoon finely chopped fresh cilantro

2 teaspoons cornstarch

2 cloves garlic, crushed through a press

½ teaspoon kosher salt

½ teaspoon freshly ground black pepper

¼ cup sugar

2 tablespoons vegetable oil

1 teaspoon Asian fish sauce (*nam pla* or *nuoc mam*)

Sriracha, or other hot red pepper sauce

4 crusty oblong French rolls, split

½ cup fresh cilantro leaves, for serving

½ medium cucumber, peeled and thinly sliced, for serving

How to make the succulent Vietnamese *banh mi* sandwich is as personal as choosing what to put on your hamburger. Some cooks include a slice of liver-y pork pâté, or substitute Korean kimchi for the pickled vegetables, or schmear the roll with mayonnaise. Here's a meatball version with a sweet-savory caramel sauce balanced by the tang of crunchy pickled root vegetables. An inexpensive plastic V-slicer juliennes the vegetables in no time. If you can't find daikon, double up on the carrots.

1. To make the pickled vegetables, whisk the rice vinegar, sugar, and salt together in a medium bowl. Add the carrots and daikon and mix. Let stand for at least 30 minutes or up to 2 hours. For longer storage, transfer to a covered container and refrigerate for up to 2 days.

2. To make the meatball mixture, combine the ground pork, shallots,

fish sauce, cilantro, cornstarch, garlic, salt, and pepper together in a medium bowl. Cover and refrigerate for at least 15 minutes or up to 4 hours.

3. To make the caramel sauce, combine the sugar and 2 tablespoons water in a medium saucepan. Cook over medium-high heat, stirring constantly, until the sugar dissolves. Cook without stirring, occasionally swirling the saucepan by its handle to combine the syrup and washing down any crystals on the inside of the saucepan with a pastry brush dipped in cold water, until the mixture caramelizes to the color of an old penny, about 3 minutes. It should be smoking and smell slightly acrid. Carefully add 1 cup hot tap water (it will splatter and harden) and stir until the caramel is dissolved. Remove from the heat.

4. Using your wet hands rinsed under cold water, shape the pork mixture into 16 equal meatballs. Transfer to a baking sheet. Heat the oil in a skillet over medium-high heat. Add the meatballs and cook, turning occasionally, until lightly browned, about 6 minutes. Add

the caramel sauce. Cook, uncovered, until the meatballs are cooked through and the sauce has reduced to about 3 tablespoons, about 6 minutes. Stir in the fish sauce and season with hot sauce. Remove from the heat and cover to keep warm.

5. For each sandwich, place 4 meatballs in a roll and drizzle with some of the caramel sauce. Drain the pickled vegetables. Top the meatballs with as much of the pickled vegetables as you wish, along with the cilantro leaves and cucumber slices. Serve warm, with the hot sauce and any remaining pickled vegetables on the side.

bbq pork meatball sandwiches
with poppy seed slaw

poppy seed slaw

2 tablespoons cider vinegar

2 tablespoons Sweet and Spicy BBQ Sauce (page 109), or your favorite store-bought sauce

2 teaspoons sugar

½ teaspoon kosher salt

½ teaspoon freshly ground black pepper

½ cup vegetable oil

1 (14-ounce) bag coleslaw mix

2 scallions, white and green parts, finely chopped

1 tablespoon poppy seeds

4 medium-sized soft oblong sandwich rolls, split lengthwise

BBQ Pork Meatballs (page 109)

Sweet and Spicy BBQ Sauce (page 109), or your favorite store-bought sauce

During the summer grilling season, my backyard Weber grill pumps out pork in all its smoky glory. My friends and family request their slow-cooked favorites, from spareribs to pulled shoulder, and now these sandwiches have joined the list. The difference is that these sandwiches deliver big flavor in much less time.

1. To make the slaw, whisk the vinegar, barbecue sauce, sugar, salt, and pepper together in a medium bowl. Gradually whisk in the oil. Add the coleslaw mix, scallions, and poppy seeds and combine. Cover and refrigerate for at least 1 hour or up to 8 hours.

2. Divide the slaw evenly on the bottoms of the sandwich rolls. Top each with 3 meatballs. Drizzle each sandwich with about 2 tablespoons of the barbecue sauce. Add the sandwich tops and serve immediately.

veal parmesan
meatball hoagies

makes 6 sandwiches

veal meatballs

1½ pounds ground veal

1 medium yellow onion, shredded on the large holes of a box grater

1 clove garlic, crushed through a press

⅔ cup dried Italian-seasoned bread crumbs

3 tablespoons dry white wine, such as Pinot Grigio

2 large eggs, beaten

1½ teaspoons kosher salt

½ teaspoon freshly ground black pepper

meatball coating

1 cup all-purpose flour

½ teaspoon kosher salt

¼ teaspoon freshly ground black pepper

3 large eggs

1 cup dried Italian-seasoned bread crumbs

2 cups olive or vegetable oil

6 crusty oblong Italian rolls, split lengthwise

6 slices mozzarella, each cut into thirds (18 pieces total)

3½ cups Everyday Tomato Sauce (page 127), or store-bought marinara sauce, heated

Freshly grated Parmesan cheese, for serving

Whether you call them hoagies, grinders, or subs, there is a lot to love in these sandwiches. The meatballs have a crusty coating around their juicy veal interior, and a cloak of melted mozzarella cheese makes a good thing better. Top with a zesty tomato sauce and you have one helluva meatball sandwich. Admittedly, this sandwich takes some effort, so simmer the tomato sauce and prepare the meatballs before coating and frying to streamline the operation.

1. To make the meatballs, mix the veal, onion, garlic, bread crumbs, wine, eggs, salt, and pepper together with your hands in a large bowl. Cover and refrigerate for at least 15 minutes or up to 2 hours.

2. Using wet hands rinsed under cold water, shape the meat mixture into 18 equal meatballs. Place on a platter. Cover and refrigerate until ready to cook, at least 15 minutes and up to 12 hours.

3. To coat and fry the meatballs, mix the flour, salt, and pepper in a shallow bowl. Beat the eggs well in another shallow bowl. Place the bread crumbs in a third shallow bowl. Line a baking sheet with parchment or wax paper.

4. One meatball at a time, roll in the flour mixture, dip in the eggs, and coat with the bread crumbs. Place on the baking sheet. Let stand for 15 minutes to set the coating.

5. Heat the olive oil in a large skillet over medium-high heat until shimmering. Place a wire cake rack over a rimmed baking sheet near the stove. In batches, add the meatballs to the hot oil and cook, turning once, until golden brown, about 3 minutes. Using a slotted spoon, transfer the meatballs to the wire rack to drain. Let the oil reheat to shimmering between batches.

6. Position the broiler rack about 6 inches from the source of heat and preheat the broiler. For each sandwich, arrange 3 meatballs in each opened roll and top with 3 pieces of mozzarella. Place on a broiler pan. Broil until the cheese melts and the edges of the rolls are toasted, about 1 minute.

7. To serve, place each sandwich on a plate and spoon ¼ cup tomato sauce over the meatballs. Transfer the remaining tomato sauce to a serving bowl. Serve hot, with the tomato sauce and Parmesan passed at the table.

pork meatball sliders with pan-roasted red peppers and provolone

makes sliders, servings

pan-roasted peppers

2 tablespoons olive oil

3 medium red bell peppers, seeded and cut into strips about 3 inches long and ½ inch wide

2 teaspoons tomato paste

1 tablespoon chopped fresh oregano

Kosher salt and freshly ground black pepper

pork meatball sliders

1 cup fresh bread crumbs

½ cup whole milk

1 pound sweet pork sausage, casings removed

8 ounces ground pork

1 medium yellow onion, shredded on the large holes of a box grater

1 clove garlic, crushed through a press

½ teaspoon kosher salt

¼ teaspoon crushed hot red pepper

18 small crusty French rolls, split crosswise

6 slices provolone cheese, each cut into thirds (18 pieces total)

There were not (and there still are not) White Castle drive-ins in my home state of California, so their popular mini-burgers were not part of my upbringing. Sliders have graduated to restaurant menus all over the country in guises that are decidedly more upscale than the original condiment-free beef and onion burgers. Here's one of my favorite versions, with the zesty Italian flavors of sausage and peppers.

1. To cook the peppers, heat the oil in a large skillet over medium heat. Add the peppers and mix well. Cook, stirring occasionally, until softened, about 10 minutes. Cover and cook, stirring occasionally, until tender, about 10 minutes longer. Dissolve the tomato paste in ¼ cup water in a small bowl. Pour into the skillet and add the oregano.

Cook over high heat, stirring often, until the liquid is reduced to about 2 tablespoons, about 2 minutes. Season with salt and pepper. Set aside.

2. To make the meatballs, combine the bread crumbs and milk in a small bowl. Let stand until the crumbs soak up the milk, about 3 minutes. Drain in a wire sieve to remove the excess milk. Transfer to a large bowl. Add the sausage, ground pork, onion, garlic, salt, and hot pepper and mix well. Cover and refrigerate for at least 15 minutes or up to 4 hours.

3. Position oven racks in the center and top third of the oven and preheat to 375°F. Lightly oil a rimmed baking sheet. Arrange the open rolls on a second baking sheet (no need to oil the sheet for the buns).

4. Using wet hands rinsed under cold water, shape the meat mixture into 18 balls. Arrange on the oiled baking sheet. Bake on the center rack until the meatballs are lightly browned, about 20 minutes. Top each meatball with a piece of provolone. Return the meatballs to the center rack. Place the baking sheet with the rolls on the top rack. Bake until the cheese on the meatballs is melted and the rolls are warmed, about 5 minutes more.

5. To serve, reheat the peppers in the skillet over medium heat. For each slider, place a meatball on the bottom half of a roll (scoop out some of the crumb to make more room for the meatball, if you wish). Add a spoonful of the pepper mixture and then the bun top. Serve warm.

open-faced meatball sandwiches with porcini sauce and ricotta

makes **4** sandwiches

meatballs

8 ounces ground round (85 percent lean)

8 ounces ground pork

1 small yellow onion, shredded on the large holes of a box grater

⅓ cup dried Italian-seasoned bread crumbs

1 large egg plus 1 large egg yolk, beaten together

1 clove garlic, crushed through a press

1¼ teaspoons kosher salt

¼ teaspoon freshly ground black pepper

With most meatball sandwiches, you have a choice of eating them out-of-hand or using a fork and knife. But this one, with a big heap of earthy mushroom sauce covering sliced meatballs on ricotta-slathered bread, absolutely requires silverware. It is miles away from a "red sauce" meatball grinder—not that there's anything wrong with that!

1. To make the meatballs, mix the ground round, ground pork, onion, bread crumbs, egg and egg yolk, garlic, salt, and pepper together in a large bowl. Cover and refrigerate for at least 15 minutes or up to 4 hours.

2. Position a rack in the center of the oven and preheat to 375°F. Lightly oil a rimmed baking sheet. Using your wet hands rinsed under cold water, shape the meat mixture into 8 large meatballs. Place on the baking sheet. Bake until the meatballs are firm enough to turn, about 15 minutes. Turn the meatballs and continue cooking until they are browned and cooked through with no sign of pink in the center, about 20 minutes longer.

3. Meanwhile, make the sauce. Combine the dried mushrooms and 2 cups water in a small saucepan, and bring to a boil over high heat. Remove from the heat and let stand until the mushrooms soften, about 20 minutes. Lift the soaked mushrooms out of the

porcini sauce

1 ounce (about 1 cup) dried porcini mushrooms, rinsed briefly under cold water to remove grit

2 tablespoons olive oil

10 ounces white mushrooms, sliced

1 small yellow onion, finely chopped

1 clove garlic, minced

1 tablespoon tomato paste

¼ teaspoon dried oregano

Kosher salt and freshly ground black pepper

8 wide slices crusty artisanal-style bread, cut about ¼ inch thick

1 clove garlic, peeled

¾ cup ricotta cheese

Chopped fresh basil or parsley, for garnish

liquid with a slotted spoon and chop coarsely. Line a wire sieve with moistened paper towels and place over a bowl. Drain the soaking liquid through the sieve, leaving any grit in the saucepan.

4. Heat the oil in a large skillet over medium heat. Add the white mushrooms and cook until they give off their moisture and are beginning to brown, about 8 minutes. Add the onion and garlic and cook until they soften, about 3 minutes. Add the reserved soaked mushrooms and the soaking liquid, tomato paste, and oregano and stir to dissolve the tomato paste. Bring to a boil and reduce the heat to medium-low. Simmer until the liquid is reduced to about ½ cup, about 15 minutes. Season with salt and pepper.

5. Position a broiler rack about 6 inches from the source of heat. Arrange the bread slices on a broiler pan and broil, turning once until toasted, about 1½ minutes. Rub one side of the slices with the garlic clove.

6. Transfer the meatballs to a carving board and slice each in half. For each serving, overlap 2 bread slices on a plate, garlic side up. Place 4 meatball halves on the bread slices. Top with one-fourth of the mushroom sauce, about 3 tablespoons of the ricotta, and a sprinkle of basil. Serve hot.

meatball hoagies
with marinara sauce

1 tablespoon olive oil

1 medium yellow onion, finely chopped

2 cloves garlic, minced

¾ cup fresh bread crumbs

¼ cup whole milk

2 pounds meat loaf mix (equal parts ground beef, ground pork, and ground veal)

½ cup (2 ounces) freshly grated Parmesan cheese, plus more for serving

1 large egg, beaten

2 tablespoons minced fresh parsley

1½ teaspoons dried oregano

1½ teaspoons kosher salt

½ teaspoon freshly ground black pepper

3½ cups Everyday Tomato Sauce (page 127) or use store-bought marinara sauce

6 oblong Italian rolls, split

I can buy meatball hoagies at my corner delicatessen, but they can't hold a candle to the ones I make in my kitchen. Most store-bought meatballs taste more like bread crumbs than meat. Not so with my homemade meatballs. To keep them tender, they simmer right in the sauce without browning. If you prefer a firmer version, brown them in olive oil first, then add to the sauce.

1. To make the meatballs, heat the oil in a small skillet over medium heat. Add the onion and cook, stirring occasionally, until tender, about 5 minutes. Stir in the garlic and cook until fragrant, about 1 minute. Transfer to a large bowl and let cool until tepid.

2. Add the bread crumbs to the bowl and sprinkle with the milk. Let stand until the bread crumbs soak up the milk, about 3 minutes. Add the meat loaf mix, Parmesan, egg, parsley, oregano, salt, and pepper and mix well.

3. Using your wet hands rinsed under cold water, shape the meat mixture into 18 equal meatballs. Place on a baking sheet.

4. Bring the tomato sauce to a simmer in a large saucepan over medium heat. Carefully add the meatballs and reduce the heat to medium-low. Simmer until the meatballs are cooked through, about 20 minutes.

5. For each hoagie, using a slotted spoon, arrange 3 meatballs in a split roll. Spoon about ¼ cup of the tomato sauce over the meatballs. Sprinkle with about 2 tablespoons of Parmesan. Serve hot, with the remaining tomato sauce passed at the table.

saucy
meatballs

beef meatball bourguignon

makes **4** to **6** servings

meatballs

¾ cup fresh bread crumbs

¼ cup whole milk

1½ pounds ground round (85 percent lean)

2 large eggs, beaten

3 tablespoons finely chopped shallots

2 tablespoons finely chopped fresh parsley

1½ teaspoons kosher salt

½ teaspoon freshly ground black pepper

When you want the classic French bistro flavors of beef bourguignon, but don't have the time for tenderizing chunks of tough meat with long simmering, make the meatball version. An Australian Shiraz is a good bet for the wine because it usually isn't aged in oak, so the sauce won't have any off, woodsy flavors. Choose among boiled new potatoes, egg noodles, or even polenta as a side dish for this ragout.

1. To make the meatballs, place the bread crumbs in a large bowl. Sprinkle with the milk and let stand until the crumbs soften, about 3 minutes. Add the ground round, eggs, shallots, parsley, salt, and pepper and mix well. Cover and refrigerate for at least 15 minutes or up to 4 hours.

2. Position a rack in the center of the oven and preheat to 375°F. Lightly oil a metal roasting pan.

3. Using your wet hands rinsed under cold water, shape the meat mixture into 18 equal meatballs. Arrange in the roasting pan and bake until lightly browned, 20 to 25 minutes.

4. Transfer the meatballs to a plate. Pour out any fat in the pan. Heat the pan over medium-high heat until sizzling. Add ½ cup water and bring to a boil, scraping up the browned bits with a wooden spatula. Remove the pan from the heat and set aside.

5. Meanwhile, start the sauce. Combine the oil and pancetta in a large saucepan over medium heat and cook, stirring occasionally, until the pancetta is browned, about 10 minutes. Using a slotted spoon, transfer the pancetta to paper towels to drain.

bourguignon sauce

1 teaspoon vegetable oil

4 ounces pancetta, coarsely chopped

10 ounces cremini mushrooms, quartered

¼ cup finely chopped shallots

3 tablespoons unsalted butter

1 medium carrot, cut into ¼-inch dice

¼ cup all-purpose flour

2 cups homemade beef stock or canned reduced-sodium beef broth

1 cup hearty red wine, such as Shiraz

2 tablespoons brandy or Cognac (optional)

2 teaspoons tomato paste

½ teaspoon dried thyme

Kosher salt and freshly ground black pepper

Chopped fresh parsley, for serving

6. Increase the heat to medium-high. Add the mushrooms to the fat in the saucepan and cook, stirring occasionally, until browned, about 7 minutes. Stir in the shallots and cook until they soften, about 2 minutes. Add the butter and let it melt. Stir in the carrot. Sprinkle with the flour and stir well. Stir in the deglazed pan juices, the broth, wine, brandy, if using, tomato paste, and thyme and bring to a boil. Reduce the heat to medium-low and simmer until lightly thickened, about 10 minutes.

7. Return the meatballs and the pancetta to the skillet and cover with the lid ajar. Cook until the carrot is tender, about 15 minutes. Season with salt and pepper. Serve hot, sprinkled with parsley.

moroccan meatball tagine
on couscous

moroccan meatballs

1 large egg

2 tablespoons tomato paste

1 pound ground lamb

1 small yellow onion, shredded on the large holes of a box grater

½ cup fresh bread crumbs

1 tablespoon finely chopped fresh cilantro or parsley

2 cloves garlic, crushed through a press

1 teaspoon kosher salt

⅛ teaspoon cayenne pepper

4 tablespoons olive oil

2 medium yellow onions, chopped

2 medium carrots, cut into ½-inch rounds

2 medium zucchini, cut into ½-inch rounds

2 cloves garlic, minced

½ teaspoon ground cinnamon

½ teaspoon ground cumin

½ teaspoon dried oregano

⅛ teaspoon cayenne pepper

1 (28-ounce) can plum tomatoes in juice, coarsely chopped, juices reserved

2 cups canned reduced-sodium chicken broth

1 (19-ounce) can garbanzo beans, drained and rinsed

Kosher salt and freshly ground black pepper

Hot cooked couscous, for serving

Chopped fresh cilantro, for garnish

Moroccan cuisine owes much of its intriguing flavors to deft combinations of piquant spices and fragrant herbs. The word "tagine" refers to both the Moroccan stew and the cooking utensil that is used to make it. While a tagine pot is a colorful addition to your kitchen (and the cone-shaped lid distributes steam to keep the meat moist during long cooking), this deliciously aromatic meatball stew can be made just as easily in a Dutch oven.

1. To make the meatballs, whisk the egg and tomato paste together in a medium bowl to dissolve the tomato paste. Add the lamb, onion, bread crumbs, cilantro, garlic, salt, and cayenne and mix well until combined. Cover and refrigerate for at least 15 minutes or up to 4 hours. Using your wet hands rinsed under cold water, shape the lamb mixture into 18 equal meatballs. Transfer to a plate.

2. Heat 2 tablespoons of the oil in a Dutch oven or flameproof casserole over medium heat. In batches, add the meatballs and cook, turning occasionally, until lightly browned, about 6 minutes. Using a slotted spoon, return the meatballs to the plate.

3. Add the remaining 2 tablespoons oil to the Dutch oven and heat. Add the onions and carrots and cook, stirring up the browned bits in the pot with a wooden spatula, until the onions are tender, about 5 minutes. Add the zucchini and garlic and cook, stirring occasionally, until the zucchini begins to soften, about 3 minutes. Stir in the cinnamon, cumin, oregano, and cayenne, then the tomatoes and their juices and the broth. Bring to a boil. Reduce the heat to medium-low and simmer, uncovered, until slightly reduced, about 15 minutes.

4. Add the meatballs and garbanzo beans and cover. Simmer until the meatballs are cooked through, about 15 minutes. Season with salt and pepper.

5. Spoon the couscous into bowls. Add the meatballs and sauce. Sprinkle with cilantro and serve hot.

FREEZING MEATBALLS

There have been countless times that I have been thankful for a hoard of meatballs stored in my freezer. Freeze naked, unsauced meatballs, and they are ready to be dressed with a freshly prepared sauce (see page 19 for some suggestions).

Generically seasoned meatballs with versatile flavors such as onion and garlic are the best ones for freezing, as they can be matched with a wide range of sauces. The mildly spiced Italian-style meatballs on pages 53 and 58, the Bourguignon meatballs on page 64, or the Swedish meatballs on page 74 all fit this description.

Cook the meatballs before freezing. Baking is best because it yields the largest amount of meatballs with the least effort and time expended. Make the meat mixture with meat that you are sure has not been previously frozen, or the meatballs will have a mealy texture. Roll the meat mixture into the number of balls recommended in the recipe, place them on an oiled baking sheet, and bake in a preheated 375°F oven until browned and cooked through, about 25 minutes. Let cool completely. (If you are a fan of grilled meatballs, any of the recipes in the Meatballs on the Grill chapter can be cooked and frozen without their sauces, although part of their appeal is their hot-off-the-grill sizzle. But, grilling is a great cooking method during hot weather when you don't want to turn on the oven.)

Arrange the cooked meatballs on a clean baking sheet and freeze until the individual meatballs are frozen solid, about 2 hours. Transfer the frozen meatballs to a plastic freezer storage bag, mark with the date of preparation, and freeze for up to 3 months. To use them, thaw in the refrigerator for a few hours before adding to the freshly prepared sauce; simmer until heated through, 10 to 15 minutes. Or, add the frozen meatballs to the sauce and simmer until thawed and heated through, about 20 minutes.

german meatballs
in caper sauce

makes **4** to **6** servings

german meatballs

1 cup fresh bread crumbs

¼ cup whole milk

2 large eggs

2 teaspoons anchovy paste

Grated zest of 1 lemon

1 teaspoon kosher salt

½ teaspoon freshly ground black pepper

1 pound ground round (85 percent lean)

8 ounces ground veal

1 medium yellow onion, shredded on the large holes of a box grater

2 tablespoons drained and rinsed nonpareil capers

1 quart homemade beef stock or canned reduced-sodium beef broth

2 bay leaves

In Germany, these tender, braised meatballs flavored with the slightly bitter accent of capers are called *Königsberger Klopse* ("meat dumplings from Königsberg"). The once-mighty capital of East Prussia is now called Kaliningrad and is in Russian territory. To help the meatballs keep their shape, chill the mixture before shaping, and then refrigerate the balls before braising. Buttered spaetzle or noodles would be a fine accompaniment.

1. To make the meatballs, combine the bread crumbs and milk in a large bowl. Let stand until the crumbs soak up the milk, about 3 minutes. Add the eggs, anchovy paste, lemon zest, salt, and pepper and whisk until the anchovy paste dissolves. Add the ground round, ground veal, onion, and capers and mix well. Cover and refrigerate for at least 30 minutes or up to 4 hours.

2. Line a rimmed baking sheet with wax paper. Using your wet hands rinsed under cold water, shape the meat mixture into 18 equal meatballs. Place the meatballs on the baking sheet, cover loosely with plastic wrap, and refrigerate for at least 30 minutes or up to 4 hours.

3. Bring the broth, 2 cups water, and the bay leaves to a boil in a large Dutch oven or flameproof casserole over high heat. Reduce the heat to medium. One at a time, reshaping them as needed, transfer the meatballs to the simmering broth mixture. They will firm up when they hit the broth. Keep the broth mixture at a

caper sauce

4 tablespoons (½ stick) unsalted butter

¼ cup all-purpose flour

½ cup sour cream

1 teaspoon anchovy paste

3 tablespoons drained and rinsed nonpareil capers

Kosher salt and freshly ground black pepper

Chopped fresh parsley, for garnish

steady simmer. Cook until the meatballs are cooked through, about 20 minutes. Using a slotted spoon, transfer the meatballs to a platter and cover with aluminum foil to keep warm.

4. Remove the Dutch oven from the heat. Skim any fat or foam from the surface. Discard the bay leaves. Measure the liquid—you should have 4 cups. If necessary, boil over high heat to reduce to 4 cups, or add water to increase to 4 cups.

5. To make the sauce, melt the butter in the Dutch oven over medium heat. Whisk in the flour and let bubble, without browning, for 1 minute. Whisk in the cooking liquid and bring to a boil over medium-high heat. Cook, whisking often, until reduced by about one-quarter, about 10 minutes. Reduce the heat to low. Add the sour cream and anchovy paste and whisk to dissolve the paste. Stir in the capers. Return the meatballs to the pot. Cover and cook until the meatballs are heated through, without letting the sauce come to a boil, about 2 minutes. Season with salt and pepper. Sprinkle with the parsley and serve hot.

meatballs in chile verde

chile verde

6 fresh mild green chiles, such as New Mexico, Anaheim, or California

2 poblano chiles

1½ pounds tomatillos, husks removed

1 medium white onion, coarsely chopped

½ cup packed chopped fresh cilantro

4 cloves garlic, coarsely chopped

1 jalapeño, seeded and coarsely chopped

3 tablespoons olive oil

3 tablespoons all-purpose flour

2 cups canned reduced-sodium chicken broth

1 teaspoon ground cumin

1 teaspoon dried oregano

1 teaspoon kosher salt

Is there a single restaurant in New Mexico that doesn't make chile verde, that green stew that will warm your insides like a glowing campfire? It's never better than when made with meatballs. My favorite way to serve it is on a bed of polenta, which gives it a tamale-like vibe.

1. To make the chile verde, position a broiler rack about 6 inches from the source of heat and preheat the broiler. Arrange the mild and poblano chiles on a broiler pan. Broil the chiles, turning occasionally, until the skins are blackened and blistered, about 10 minutes. Transfer to a bowl and let cool until easy to handle. Discard the skins, seeds, and ribs, and coarsely chop the chiles. Set aside.

2. Bring a large saucepan of salted water to a boil over high heat. Add the tomatillos and reduce the heat to medium. Simmer until the tomatillos turn uniformly olive green and soften, but do not burst, about 5 minutes. Using a slotted spoon, transfer the tomatillos to a bowl. Add the onion, cilantro, garlic, and jalapeño and mix to combine. In batches, transfer the mixture to a blender and puree with the lid ajar (to create a vent and release the steam from the hot tomatillos).

3. Heat the oil in a Dutch oven or covered casserole over medium heat. Whisk in the flour and cook until very lightly browned, about 1 minute. Whisk in the reserved chopped chiles, the tomatillo puree, broth, cumin, oregano, and salt. Bring to boil. Reduce the heat to

meatballs

12 ounces ground round (85 percent lean)

12 ounces ground pork

½ cup crushed tortilla chips

2 large eggs, beaten

1 medium yellow onion, shredded on the large holes of a box grater

2 cloves garlic, crushed through a press

1¼ teaspoons kosher salt, pus more as needed

1 teaspoon ground cumin

1 teaspoon dried oregano

¼ teaspoon freshly ground black pepper

3 tablespoons olive oil

Hot cooked polenta, for serving

medium-low. Simmer, uncovered and stirring occasionally, until reduced by about one-quarter, about 45 minutes.

4. Meanwhile, make the meatballs. Mix the ground round, ground pork, tortilla chips, eggs, onion, garlic, salt, cumin, oregano, and pepper together in a large bowl. Cover and refrigerate for at least 15 minutes or up to 4 hours.

5. Using your wet hands rinsed under cold water, shape the meat mixture into 24 equal meatballs. Transfer the meatballs to a platter. Heat the oil in a large nonstick skillet over medium heat. In batches, add the meatballs to the skillet and cook, turning occasionally, until lightly browned, about 6 minutes. Return the browned meatballs to the platter.

6. Add the meatballs to the *chile verde*. Cover, with the lid ajar, and cook until the meatballs are cooked through, about 15 minutes. Season the chile with salt. Serve hot, spooned over polenta.

swedish meatballs
with lingonberry sauce

meatballs

12 ounces ground round (85 percent lean)

12 ounces ground pork

¾ cup crushed rye crackers (see Note)

½ cup heavy cream

1 medium yellow onion, shredded on the large holes of a box grater

2 large eggs, beaten

1½ teaspoons kosher salt

¾ teaspoon ground allspice

¾ teaspoon freshly ground black pepper

2 tablespoons vegetable oil

easy brown sauce

2 tablespoons unsalted butter

2 tablespoons all-purpose flour

2 cups homemade beef stock or canned reduced-sodium beef broth

Kosher salt and freshly ground black pepper

Lingonberry sauce, for serving

There is no single authentic recipe for Swedish meatballs any more than there is one for Italian meatballs. This rendition has elements from various recipes, including heavy cream for extra moisture and tenderness and ground allspice and crushed rye crackers for an interesting "can't quite place" seasoning. Boiled new potatoes are the classic accompaniment, but I sure like these on egg noodles. Look for tangy lingonberry sauce at specialty grocers or your local IKEA.

1. To make the meatballs, combine the ground round, ground pork, cracker crumbs, heavy cream, onion, eggs, salt, allspice, and pepper in a large bowl and mix well. Cover and refrigerate for at least 15 minutes or up to 4 hours. Using your hands rinsed under cold water, shape the mixture into about 32 equal small meatballs. Transfer to a baking sheet.

2. Heat the vegetable oil in a large nonstick skillet over medium heat. In batches, add the meatballs and cook, turning occasionally, until browned on all sides, about 6 minutes. Using a slotted spoon, return to the baking sheet. Pour out the fat, but not the browned bits, in the skillet.

3. To make the sauce, add the butter to the skillet and melt over medium heat. Whisk in the flour, reduce the heat to medium-low, and let bubble without browning for 1 minute. Whisk in the broth and bring to a simmer over medium heat. Return the meatballs to the skillet, cover with the lid ajar, and return the heat to medium-low. Simmer until the sauce is lightly thickened and the meatballs are cooked through, about 15 minutes. Season with salt and pepper and serve hot with the lingonberry sauce.

NOTE: Somewhat dark, very crispy rye crackers are also known as rusks. To crush them, crumble up some crackers and process in a food processor. Or place the crackers in a sturdy plastic bag and crush with a rolling pin.

FREEZING MEATBALLS IN SAUCE

When testing recipes for this book, there were inevitably leftovers. To store the overflow, my chest freezer was never put to better use. For months afterwards, when I was at a loss for what to cook for dinner, or I was in the mood for hot homemade soup for lunch, all I had to do was retrieve a container from the freezer.

The best meatball recipes for freezing have the balls cooked directly in the sauce or broth and use meat that has not been previously frozen for making the meat mixture. The meatballs can be browned in a skillet or oven before adding to the sauce. Skip deep-fried or steamed meatballs, or ones with a crispy coating, and keep in mind that fish-based balls are often too delicate for successful freezing. If the sauce includes yogurt or sour cream, expect it to curdle slightly when reheated, although in my recipes, I usually add cornstarch to the dairy products to discourage curdling. Of course, with pasta dishes, the pasta should be cooked just before serving and served on the side.

Using a slotted spoon, transfer the cooked and cooled meatballs to airtight covered microwave-safe containers. I prefer 1-quart containers, as they conveniently hold enough for two servings—if the storage container is too large, the meatballs will take a long time to thaw. Add enough sauce to completely cover the meatballs, adding an appropriate broth or even water if needed to submerge the balls. Close the container and identify the contents with an indelible pen and the date of preparation. Freeze for up to 3 months.

The easiest way to serve frozen meatballs is to microwave the covered container of meatballs and sauce at 50 percent (Medium) powder until the sauce has thawed and the meatballs are hot, 20 to 30 minutes, depending on the wattage of your microwave and the size of the container. Occasionally check the progress, stirring the meatballs and sauce as they defrost. If you wish, once the meatballs and sauce have begun to thaw (after 10 minutes or so), transfer them to a shallow microwave-safe baking dish, separating the meatballs in the process. Cover tightly with plastic wrap, and continue the reheating.

As an alternative, thaw the meatballs and sauce first in the refrigerator for at least 12 hours, then reheat, covered, in a heavy-bottomed large saucepan over medium-low heat, stirring occasionally, until hot, 10 to 15 minutes.

Here are some sauced meatball recipes in this book that freeze well:

danish meatballs
in cream sauce

1 pound ground veal

1 pound ground pork

1 small onion, shredded on the large holes of a box grater

1 large egg, beaten

Kosher salt and freshly ground black pepper

½ cup all-purpose flour

About ½ cup club soda, as needed

2 tablespoons unsalted butter

2 tablespoons vegetable oil, plus more as needed

1½ cups heavy cream

Chopped fresh parsley, dill, or chives, for garnish

Danish cooks hold the right to claim the most tender meatballs, *frikadeller*. Pork and veal keep them delicate, and a plentiful amount of club soda adds moisture. At first, the soda will seem difficult to incorporate, but add it gradually, and the mixture will soak it up. With a very simple cream sauce made from the pan juices, the meatballs are a culinary equivalent of Scandinavian furniture: Their simplicity belies a deeper aesthetic. Serve with braised red cabbage and boiled new potatoes with parsley.

1. Combine the ground veal, ground pork, onion, egg, 2 teaspoons salt, and ½ teaspoon pepper in a large bowl. Using your hands, gently but thoroughly mix the ingredients, sprinkling in the flour as you work, until barely combined. A tablespoon at a time, gradually mix in enough of the club soda to make a mixture that is very moist but firm enough to hold its shape. Cover and refrigerate for at least 30 minutes or up to 4 hours.

2. Using your wet hands rinsed under cold water, shape the mixture into 24 equal meatballs. Transfer to a baking sheet. Cover loosely with plastic wrap and refrigerate for at least 30 minutes or up to 8 hours.

3. Heat the butter and oil together in a large skillet over medium heat. In batches, add the meatballs and cook, turning occasionally, until lightly browned on all sides and cooked through, about 12 minutes, adding more oil as needed. Transfer to a plate and tent with aluminum foil to keep warm.

4. Pour off the fat, but not the browned bits, in the skillet. Add the cream to the skillet and bring to a boil over high heat, stirring up the browned bits with a wooden spatula. Boil until lightly thickened, about 5 minutes. Season with salt and pepper. Return the meatballs to the skillet, reduce the heat to low, and stir gently, just to coat them with the sauce. Simmer for 1 minute to reheat the meatballs.

5. Transfer the meatballs to a serving bowl, sprinkle with parsley, and serve hot.

koftas with dill

makes **4** to **6** servings

dill meatballs

1½ pounds ground round (85 percent lean)

1 medium yellow onion, shredded on the large holes of a box grater

2 large eggs, beaten

2 tablespoons chopped fresh dill

2 tablespoons chopped fresh parsley

2 cloves garlic, crushed through a press

1¾ teaspoons kosher salt

½ teaspoon ground allspice

½ teaspoon ground cinnamon

½ teaspoon freshly ground black pepper

2 tablespoons olive oil

The hint of allspice and cinnamon in the meatballs gives this recipe away as Middle Eastern, especially in combination with the highly aromatic dill. Every summer, great bushes of dill volunteer in my garden, and this recipe helps me make use of my bounty. This dish is at its best when spooned over basmati rice.

1. To make the meatballs, combine the ground round, onion, eggs, dill, parsley, garlic, salt, allspice, cinnamon, and pepper and mix well. Cover and refrigerate for at least 15 minutes or up to 4 hours. Using your wet hands rinsed under cold water, shape the meat mixture into 18 equal meatballs. Transfer to a plate.

2. Heat 2 tablespoons of oil in a large nonstick skillet over medium heat. In batches, without crowding, add the meatballs and cook, turning occasionally, until lightly browned, about 6 minutes. Using a slotted spoon, return the meatballs to the plate. Pour out the fat, but not the browned bits, in the skillet.

3. To make the sauce, add the oil to the skillet and heat over medium heat. Add the onion and cook, stirring occasionally, until softened, about 5 minutes, scraping up the browned bits with a wooden spoon. Stir in the garlic and cook until fragrant, about 1 minute. Add the tomato puree and bring to a boil. Reduce the heat to medium-low and simmer for 10 minutes.

sauce

2 tablespoons olive oil

1 large yellow onion, chopped

2 cloves garlic, minced

1 (28-ounce) can tomato puree

2 tablespoons chopped fresh dill, plus more for garnish

Kosher salt and freshly ground black pepper

Hot cooked rice or orzo, for serving

Plain yogurt, for serving

Chopped fresh dill, for garnish

4. Stir the dill into the sauce, then add the meatballs. Bring to a simmer over high heat. Reduce the heat to medium-low. Cover the skillet with the lid ajar. Simmer until the meatballs are cooked through, about 20 minutes. Season with salt and pepper.

5. Spoon the rice into bowls and add the meatballs and sauce. Top each with a dollop of yogurt and a sprinkle of chopped dill and serve hot.

lion's head meatballs
with napa cabbage

makes **4** to **6** servings

lion's head meatballs

1 pound ground pork

1 scallion, white and green parts, minced

2 tablespoons cornstarch

¼ cup drained and minced canned water chestnuts

1 large egg, beaten

1 tablespoon peeled and shredded fresh ginger (use the large holes on a box grater)

1 tablespoon soy sauce

1 tablespoon dry sherry

2 teaspoons Asian dark sesame oil, plus more for serving

1 clove garlic, crushed through a press

¾ teaspoon kosher salt

¼ teaspoon freshly ground black pepper

4 tablespoons vegetable oil

3 tablespoons cornstarch

2 cloves garlic, minced

1 (1¾-pound) napa cabbage, cored and cut crosswise into 1½-inch-wide strips

½ cup canned reduced-sodium chicken broth

3 tablespoons soy sauce, plus more for serving

½ teaspoon sugar

Kosher salt and freshly ground black pepper

Hot cooked rice, for serving

This is a gently flavored dish that reminds me of the Cantonese Chinese restaurants of my youth, before I became enamored of spicy Szechuan and Hunan cuisines. The big pork meatball nestled in a bed of leafy greens is said to resemble a lion's head and its mane. You can use your favorite Asian green (bok choy is also good), but I prefer the mild, sweet flavor of napa cabbage.

1. To make the meatballs, combine the ground pork, scallion, cornstarch, water chestnuts, egg, ginger, soy sauce, sherry, sesame oil, crushed garlic, salt, and pepper in a large bowl and mix well. Cover and refrigerate for at least 15 minutes or up to 4 hours. Using your wet hands rinsed under cold water, shape the pork mixture into 8 equal large meatballs. Transfer to a plate.

2. Heat 2 tablespoons of the oil in a large nonstick skillet over medium heat. Put the cornstarch in a shallow bowl. Roll each meatball in the cornstarch, shaking off the excess, and place in the skillet. Cook, turning occasionally, until lightly browned on all sides, about 6 minutes. Using a slotted spoon, return the meatballs to the plate.

3. Add the remaining 2 tablespoons oil and the garlic to the skillet and stir until fragrant, about 30 seconds. In batches, stir in the cabbage and cook until wilted. Add the broth, soy sauce, and sugar and bring to a boil. Nestle the meatballs in the cabbage. Reduce the heat to medium-low and cover. Simmer until the meatballs are cooked through and the cabbage is tender, about 15 minutes. Season with salt and pepper.

4. Spoon the meatballs, cabbage mixture, and cooking liquid into shallow bowls. Sprinkle with minced scallion and drizzle with sesame oil. Serve hot, with the rice and additional soy sauce passed on the side.

persian meatballs in pomegranate and walnut sauce

makes to servings

persian meatballs

1½ pounds ground round (85 percent lean)

1 medium yellow onion, shredded on the large holes of a box grater

¼ cup dried plain bread crumbs

1 large egg, beaten

1¾ teaspoons kosher salt

½ teaspoon freshly ground black pepper

pomegranate and walnut sauce

1 quart pomegranate juice (see Note)

2 cups (8 ounces) walnut pieces

4 tablespoons vegetable oil

2 medium yellow onions, chopped

1 teaspoon ground turmeric

1 teaspoon sugar, or more to taste

2 tablespoons tomato paste

Kosher salt and freshly ground black pepper

Hot cooked basmati rice, for serving

Chopped fresh cilantro or parsley, for garnish

I first noticed these sweet-and-sour meatballs (called *fesenjan*) on the menu of a modest storefront Persian restaurant, Honey, in Teaneck, New Jersey, an area with a large Middle Eastern community. The dish was as delicious as it sounded, although the sauce was on the sweet side, to suit the cook's Persian palate. My version is a bit more savory, with the option to add more sugar if you wish. In any case, *fesenjan* is quite rich, so serve it with plenty of basmati rice to soak up the sauce. And although tasty, it is not pretty, so break up the brown-on-brown color scheme with a garnish of chopped fresh cilantro or parsley.

1. To make the meatballs, combine the ground round, onion, bread crumbs, egg, salt, and pepper in a large bowl and mix well. Cover and refrigerate for at least 15 minutes or up to 4 hours.

2. Meanwhile, to start the sauce, bring the pomegranate juice to a boil in a large saucepan over high heat. Boil until reduced to 2 cups, about 20 minutes. (The juice can also be reduced in a large microwave-safe bowl in a microwave oven on high, taking care that the juice doesn't boil over. It should take about 10 minutes, depending on the wattage of the oven.)

3. Position a rack in the center of the oven and preheat to 350°F. Spread the walnuts on a rimmed baking sheet. Bake until the walnuts are lightly toasted, about 10 minutes. Let cool. Transfer to a food processor and pulse about 10 times, until the walnuts are the consistency of coarse bread crumbs.

4. Using your wet hands rinsed under cold water, shape the meat mixture into about 24 equal meatballs. Heat 2 tablespoons of the oil in a large nonstick skillet over medium heat. In batches, add the meatballs and cook, turning occasionally, until browned on all sides, about 6 minutes. Using a slotted spoon, transfer to a plate. Pour out the fat, but not the browned bits, in the skillet.

5. Add the remaining 2 tablespoons oil to the skillet and heat over medium heat. Add the onions and cook, stirring often, until golden brown, about 12 minutes. Stir in the turmeric and sugar. Add the reduced pomegranate juice and tomato paste and stir to dissolve the tomato paste. Stir in the ground walnuts and bring to a simmer. Reduce the heat to medium-low and cook, uncovered and stirring occasionally, until the liquid is lightly thickened, about 20 minutes. (If you wish, make the sauce in a separate skillet while browning the meatballs.)

6. Add the meatballs and simmer until cooked through, about 15 minutes. (Or pour the walnut sauce into the skillet. Bring to a simmer, scraping up the browned bits in the skillet, and simmer until the meatballs are cooked through, about 15 minutes.) Season with salt and pepper.

7. Spoon the rice into bowls. Top with the meatballs and sauce and a sprinkling of cilantro. Serve hot.

NOTE: Pomegranate juice is available at supermarkets, but it is most reasonably priced at Middle Eastern grocers. Be sure to buy unsweetened 100 percent pomegranate juice without added fruit juices or flavors.

beef meatballs with horseradish sauce

meatballs

1 cup fresh rye bread crumbs

⅓ cup milk

1½ pounds ground round (85 percent lean)

2 scallions, white and pale green parts only, minced (reserve the dark green tops for garnish)

2 tablespoons drained prepared horseradish

2 large egg yolks, beaten

1½ teaspoons kosher salt

½ teaspoon caraway seeds, ground in a mortar or spice grinder (optional)

¼ teaspoon freshly ground black pepper

2 tablespoons vegetable oil

horseradish sauce

2 tablespoons unsalted butter

2 tablespoons all-purpose flour

1¾ cups homemade beef stock or canned reduced-sodium beef broth

¼ cup whole milk

½ cup sour cream

2 tablespoons drained prepared horseradish

Kosher salt and freshly ground black pepper

Chopped scallions, green tops only, for garnish

The bold flavor of horseradish is front and center in this creamy dish. Make it when you have rye bread in the house, as rye crumbs have a tanginess that matches the forthright zing of the horseradish. I can never decide on serving these with mashed potatoes, noodles, or spaetzle, so take your pick.

1. To make the meatballs, stir the bread crumbs and milk together in a large bowl and let stand until the crumbs soak up the milk, about 3 minutes. Add the ground round, scallions, horseradish, yolks, salt, caraway seeds, and pepper and mix well. Cover and refrigerate for at least 15 minutes or up to 4 hours.

2. Using your wet hands rinsed under cold water, shape the meat mixture into 18 equal meatballs. Transfer to a plate. Heat the oil in a large nonstick skillet over medium heat. Add the meatballs to the skillet and cook, turning occasionally, until lightly browned, about 6 minutes. Return to the plate.

3. To make the sauce, pour out the fat, but not the browned bits, in the skillet. Add the butter to the skillet and melt over medium-low heat. Whisk in the flour and let the mixture bubble without browning for 1 minute. Whisk in the broth and milk. Return the meatballs to the skillet and bring to a simmer over medium heat. Cover and simmer for 10 minutes. Uncover and simmer until the liquid has reduced slightly and the meatballs are cooked through, about 5 minutes more.

4. Using a slotted spoon, transfer the meatballs to a serving bowl. Whisk the sour cream and horseradish into the sauce and heat for about 30 seconds, until hot but not boiling. Season with salt and pepper. Pour the sauce over the meatballs, sprinkle with the scallion tops, and serve hot.

lamb meatballs
in green curry sauce

lamb meatballs

1 pound ground lamb

½ cup fresh bread crumbs

1 large egg, beaten

1 teaspoon ground cumin

½ teaspoon garam masala

½ teaspoon kosher salt

green curry sauce

1 tablespoon vegetable oil

1 medium yellow onion, chopped

4 cloves garlic, minced

2 tablespoons peeled and minced fresh ginger

1 jalapeño or serrano chile, seeded and minced

1 (13½-ounce) can coconut milk (do not shake)

1 teaspoon ground cumin

½ teaspoon garam masala

1 cup packed chopped cilantro leaves

1 teaspoon tamarind concentrate (sold at Indian grocers) or fresh lemon juice

Kosher salt

While flipping through an Australian food magazine, my eyes were drawn to the appetizing green sauce in a photo of Indian-style meatballs. I am one of those people who do not rate cilantro as my favorite herb, but when I developed this dish to replicate the recipe at home, the sauce proved as delicious as it was attractive. Cook some basmati rice to serve with the meatballs.

1. To make the meatballs, mix the ground lamb, bread crumbs, egg, cumin, garam masala, and salt together in a large bowl. Cover and refrigerate for at least 15 minutes or up to 4 hours.

2. To make the sauce, heat the oil in a large saucepan over medium heat. Add the onion, garlic, ginger, and chile and stir well. Open the can of coconut milk. Spoon out and measure ½ cup of the thick coconut milk that has risen to the top.

Add to the saucepan with the cumin and garam masala. Cook until the onion mixture is softened and the coconut milk is reduced and looks oily, about 5 minutes. Add 1 cup water, the cilantro, tamarind concentrate, and remaining coconut milk (about 1¼ cups). Whisk well and bring to a simmer. Reduce the heat to medium-low and cook, whisking occasionally, until slightly reduced, about 10 minutes.

3. Using your hands rinsed under cold water, shape the meat mixture into 24 equal small meatballs. Transfer to a plate. Carefully add the meatballs to the simmering sauce and cover with the lid ajar. Simmer until the sauce is thickened and the meatballs are cooked through with no sign of pink, about 20 minutes. Season with salt. Serve hot.

lamb meatballs in
spinach-coriander sauce

lamb meatballs

1 pound ground lamb

½ cup fresh bread crumbs

¼ cup plain yogurt

1 large egg, beaten

1 small yellow onion, shredded on the large holes of a box grater

2 cloves garlic, crushed through a press

1 teaspoon kosher salt

½ teaspoon ground coriander seeds

½ teaspoon ground cumin

⅛ teaspoon cayenne pepper

2 tablespoons vegetable oil

spinach-coriander sauce

1 tablespoon vegetable oil

1 medium yellow onion, chopped

2 cloves garlic, minced

1 teaspoon ground coriander seeds

20 ounces fresh spinach, tough stems removed, leaves coarsely chopped and washed (but not dried)

Kosher salt and freshly ground black pepper

Hot cooked basmati rice, for serving

Plain yogurt, for serving

The inspiration for this dish comes from the cooking of the eastern Mediterranean, where fragrant coriander seeds are used as much as the green leaves of the plant. (American cooks make a distinction, calling the seeds coriander and the leaves cilantro, but other cultures aren't as particular.) Fresh spinach, tangy yogurt, and rich lamb all combine with the coriander seeds to make this an out-of-the-ordinary meatball supper.

1. To make the meatballs, combine the lamb, bread crumbs, yogurt, egg, onion, garlic, salt, coriander, cumin, and cayenne in a large bowl and mix well. Cover and refrigerate for at least 15 minutes or up to 4 hours. Using wet hands rinsed under cold water, shape the lamb mixture into 16 equal meatballs and transfer to a baking sheet.

2. Heat the oil in a large nonstick skillet over medium heat. In batches, add the meatballs and cook, turning occasionally, until lightly browned, about 6 minutes. Using a slotted spoon, return the meatballs to the baking sheet.

3. To make the sauce, pour out all but 1 tablespoon of the fat from the skillet. Add the oil to the skillet and heat over medium heat. Add the onion and cook, stirring often, until tender, about 5 minutes. Stir in the garlic and coriander seeds and cook until fragrant, about 1 minute. In batches, add the spinach, letting each batch wilt before adding the next.

4. Add the meatballs to the skillet and cover. Reduce the heat to medium-low and simmer until the meatballs are cooked through, about 10 minutes. Season with salt and pepper. Spoon the rice into bowls and add the meatballs and spinach sauce. Top each serving with a dollop of yogurt and serve hot.

chicken teriyaki meatballs

makes **4** servings

chicken meatballs

1 pound ground chicken

½ cup panko (Japanese bread crumbs)

1 large egg, beaten

1 scallion, minced, plus more for garnish

1 tablespoon cornstarch

1 tablespoon peeled and shredded fresh ginger (use the large holes of a box grater)

1 tablespoon Japanese-style soy sauce (see Note)

½ teaspoon kosher salt

¼ teaspoon freshly ground black pepper

8 quarter-sized slices peeled fresh ginger, crushed under the flat side of a large knife, for the cooking liquid

teriyaki sauce

⅔ cup Japanese-style soy sauce (see Note)

⅔ cup mirin

⅓ cup sugar

1 tablespoon rice vinegar

Hot cooked rice, for serving

Teriyaki is a combination of two Japanese words, *teri* for "luster" and *yaki* for "grilled" or "broiled." These light-as-a-feather chicken meatballs are poached, with a sweet and shiny sauce for the teriyaki angle. I've given a variation for a grilled version, but I love how these can be poached and ready for serving in a few minutes, and their juicy, delicate texture is a revelation. Mirin, sweetened Japanese rice wine, is available at Asian grocers and many supermarkets.

1. To make the meatballs, combine the chicken, panko, egg, scallion, cornstarch, shredded ginger, soy sauce, salt, and pepper in a large bowl and mix well. Cover and refrigerate for at least 15 minutes or up to 4 hours.

2. Bring 2 quarts water and the sliced ginger to a boil in a pot over high heat. Reduce the heat to medium-low to keep at a simmer.

3. Using your wet hands rinsed under cold water, shape the chicken mixture into 20 equal meatballs. Transfer to a baking sheet. Carefully add the balls to the pot. Simmer until cooked through, about 6 minutes.

4. While the balls are cooking, make the teriyaki sauce. Bring the soy sauce, mirin, sugar, and rice vinegar to a boil in a medium saucepan over high heat. Boil until thickened and reduced to about 2/3 cup, about 5 minutes. Pour into a small bowl.

5. Using a wire spider or sieve, remove the meatballs from the cooking liquid. Drain briefly on paper towels. Spoon the rice into serving bowls. Top with the meatballs and drizzle with the sauce. Sprinkle with minced scallion and serve hot.

NOTE: There are literally hundreds of brands of Chinese soy sauce and it is easy to get one that is too salty or has off flavors. Kikkoman, the most common supermarket brand, is owned by a Japanese company but made in America, and is very reliable.

Grilled Chicken Teriyaki Meatballs:

Because the chicken mixture is soft, these meatballs are best grilled in a metal meatball-grilling basket. Prepare a medium-hot fire in an outdoor grill. Oil 20 molds in 2 baskets and place the meatballs in the baskets. Grill, covered, turning after 3 minutes, until the meatballs are browned and cooked through, about 8 minutes.

meatballs stroganoff

meatballs

1½ pounds ground round (85 percent lean)

½ cup dried plain bread crumbs

1 large egg, beaten

2 tablespoons chopped fresh dill (optional)

1¾ teaspoons kosher salt

½ teaspoon freshly ground black pepper

2 tablespoons vegetable oil

This old-fashioned recipe is a prime example of meatballs as classic comfort food. Served over egg noodles and sprinkled with fresh dill to give them a refreshing touch of green, they have provided succor and sustenance to me on many an evening when the day's events called for a meal that was both tasty and nostalgic. The dill is entirely optional, but fresh herbs keep the dish from stodginess, so substitute parsley if dill isn't handy.

1. To make the meatballs, mix the ground round, bread crumbs, egg, dill, if using, salt, and pepper together in a large bowl. Cover and refrigerate for at least 15 minutes or up to 4 hours. Using your wet hands rinsed under cold water, shape the mixture into 18 equal meatballs. Transfer to a plate.

2. Heat the oil in a large skillet over medium heat. In batches, add the meatballs and cook, turning occasionally, until lightly browned on all sides, about 6 minutes. Return to the plate. Pour off the fat, but not the browned bits, in the skillet.

3. To make the sauce, add the butter to the skillet and melt over medium-high heat. Add the mushrooms and cook, stirring occasionally, until beginning to brown, about 7 minutes. Stir in the shallots and cook, stirring occasionally, until softened, about 2 minutes. Sprinkle in the flour and stir well. Stir in the stock and bring to a simmer.

4. Return the meatballs to the skillet. Reduce the heat to medium-low and simmer until the meatballs are cooked through, about 15 minutes.

mushroom sauce

2 tablespoons unsalted butter

10 ounces cremini mushrooms, sliced

3 tablespoons finely chopped shallots

3 tablespoons all-purpose flour

2½ cups homemade beef stock or canned reduced-sodium beef broth

½ cup sour cream

2 teaspoons cornstarch

Kosher salt and freshly ground black pepper

Chopped fresh dill, for serving (optional)

5. Using a slotted spoon, transfer the meatballs to a serving bowl. Whisk the sour cream and cornstarch together in a small bowl. Whisk into the skillet and cook, whisking often, just until simmering. Season the sauce with salt and pepper. Pour over the meatballs. Sprinkle with the dill, if using. Serve hot.

meatballs
on the grill

grilled lamb meatballs on shepherd's salad with yogurt-tahini sauce

yogurt-tahini sauce

1 cup plain yogurt

2 tablespoons tahini

2 tablespoons chopped fresh mint

1 tablespoon fresh lemon juice

Kosher salt and freshly ground black pepper

lamb meatballs

1 pound ground lamb

½ cup fresh bread crumbs

1 small yellow onion, shredded on the large holes of a box grater

1 large clove garlic, crushed through a press

1 large egg, beaten

1 tablespoon plus 1 teaspoon chopped fresh mint

1½ teaspoons ground cumin

1 teaspoon kosher salt

These wonderfully seasoned lamb meatballs are a favorite summertime lunch at my house. They are served on shepherd's salad, a refreshing and chunky mix of cucumbers, tomatoes, and feta cheese that is served throughout the Middle East. The meatballs and salad can be tucked into pita as a sandwich—or simply spear the meatballs with toothpicks and serve them with the sauce as a dip (without the salad) as an appetizer.

1. To make the sauce, whisk the yogurt, tahini, mint, and lemon juice together in a serving bowl. Season with salt and pepper. Let stand at room temperature for 30 minutes to 2 hours.

2. To make the meatballs, mix the ground lamb, bread crumbs, onion, garlic, egg, mint, cumin, salt, hot pepper, cinnamon, and cloves in a large bowl. Cover and refrigerate for at least 15 minutes or up to 4 hours.

3. Prepare a medium-hot fire in an outdoor grill. Using your wet hands rinsed under cold water, shape the meat mixture into 12 equal meatballs.

4. Just before grilling the meatballs, make the salad. Toss the tomatoes, cucumber, and red onion together in a serving bowl. Drizzle with the lemon juice, then the oil, and toss. Add the feta. Season with salt and pepper. Set aside at room temperature.

¼ teaspoon crushed hot
red pepper

⅛ teaspoon ground
cinnamon

Pinch of ground cloves

shepherd's salad

2 large ripe tomatoes,
seeded and cut into
½-inch dice

1 large cucumber, peeled,
seeded, and cut into
½-inch dice

¼ cup finely chopped
red onion

1 tablespoon fresh
lemon juice

¼ cup extra virgin olive oil

½ cup (2 ounces) crumbled
feta cheese

Kosher salt and freshly
ground black pepper

Toasted pita bread,
for serving

5. To grill the meatballs with a grilling basket, lightly oil the molds (a pump oil sprayer works best). Place the meatballs in the basket and close the basket. Place the basket on the cooking grate and cover. Grill the meatballs until the undersides are lightly browned, about 3 minutes. Flip the baskets over and grill until the other sides are lightly browned and the meatballs are medium-rare, about 3 minutes more. Remove the meatballs from the baskets. Transfer to a platter.

To grill the meatballs without the baskets, lightly oil the cooking grate. Place the meatballs on the grill and cover. Grill until the undersides are lightly browned, about 3 minutes. Flip the meatballs and grill until the other sides are lightly browned and the meatballs are medium-rare, about 3 minutes. Transfer to a platter.

6. Divide the salad among 4 shallow bowls, top each with 3 meatballs, and serve with pita. Pass the sauce on the side.

grilled cheese-stuffed
meatball sliders

meatball sliders

1 pound ground round
(85 percent lean)

⅓ cup dried plain
bread crumbs

1 large egg, beaten

1 teaspoon kosher salt

¼ teaspoon freshly ground
black pepper

12 (½-inch) cubes sharp
Cheddar cheese, cut from
brick cheese

12 store-bought slider buns
or small Parker House rolls,
split

2 leaves red-leaf lettuce, torn
into 12 pieces

12 dill pickle slices (optional)

Tomato ketchup

Here is the all-American cheeseburger, transformed into a meatball. As miniature versions of a bigger food item, sliders could share "the cute factor" with cupcakes. Adorability aside, I appreciate how they deliver so many elements in a couple of bites—meat, bun, and more in a compact and delicious package.

1. To make the meatball sliders, mix the ground round, bread crumbs, egg, salt, and pepper together in a large bowl. Cover and refrigerate for at least 15 minutes or up to 4 hours.

2. Prepare a medium-hot fire in an outdoor grill. Using your wet hands rinsed under cold water, shape the meat mixture into 12 equal meatballs. One at a time, flatten a ball slightly in your palms and completely wrap a cheese cube in the meat mixture. Transfer to a plate.

3. Scoop out some of the crumb from each bun to make more room for the meatballs. (Save the crumbs for another use, such as using in meatball recipes.) Set the buns aside.

4. To grill the meatballs with a basket, lightly oil the molds (a pump sprayer works best). Place the meatballs in the basket and close it. Place the basket on the cooking grate and cover. Grill the meatballs until the undersides are lightly browned, about 3 minutes. Flip the basket over and grill until the other sides are lightly browned and the meatballs are medium-rare, about 3 minutes more. Remove the meatballs from the basket. Transfer to a platter.

To grill the meatballs without the basket, lightly oil the cooking grate. Place the meatballs on the grill and cover. Grill until the undersides are lightly browned, about 3 minutes. Flip the meatballs and grill until the other sides are lightly browned and the meatballs are medium-rare, about 3 minutes. Transfer to a platter.

5. Place the buns on the grill and grill, turning once, until lightly toasted, about 1 minute. For each slider, place a meatball on a bun bottom and top with a piece of lettuce and a pickle slice. Add a dollop of ketchup. Add the bun top and serve warm.

lemongrass-chicken meatballs
on rice vermicelli

dipping sauce

¼ cup granulated sugar

¼ cup fish sauce (*nam pla* or *nuoc mam*)

¼ cup distilled white or rice vinegar

4 cloves garlic, minced

½ carrot, shredded on the large holes of a box grater

2 Thai bird or serrano chiles, seeded and minced

vermicelli and scallion oil

10 ounces thin rice vermicelli

3 tablespoons vegetable oil

2 cloves garlic, chopped

6 scallions, white and green parts, thinly sliced

lemongrass-chicken meatballs

1 stalk lemongrass

1 pound ground chicken

1½ tablespoons minced shallots

1 tablespoon fish sauce (*nam pla* or *nuoc mam*)

1 tablespoon cornstarch

1 Thai bird or serrano chile, seeded and minced

1 clove garlic, minced

1 teaspoon light brown sugar

½ teaspoon kosher salt

My first New York restaurant job was at an American restaurant with a Thai chef. Thanks to him, I learned about Southeast Asian cooking well before its current popularity. One of his specialties was grilled lemongrass chicken, and I've adapted its flavors to these meatballs, served as they might be in Vietnam, on a bed of rice vermicelli with a tangy dipping sauce.

1. To make the dipping sauce, bring ½ cup water and the granulated sugar to a boil in a small saucepan over high heat, stirring to dissolve the sugar. Pour into a bowl and let cool. Add the fish sauce, vinegar, garlic, carrot, and chiles and stir well.

2. To prepare the vermicelli, place in a medium bowl and add enough hot tap water to cover. Let stand until the vermicelli is tender, about 10 minutes. Drain and rinse under cold running water. Drain again and return to the bowl. Toss with 1 teaspoon of the vegetable oil.

3. To make the scallion oil, pour the remaining vegetable oil into a medium skillet. Add the garlic and cook over medium heat, stirring often, until softened but not browned, about 2 minutes. Add the scallions and cook, stirring often, until wilted, about 2 minutes. Remove from the heat.

4. To make the meatballs, remove and discard the outer layers from the lemongrass to reveal the pale yellow inner stalk. Trim off the bulbous tip of the stalk. Using a very sharp knife, thinly slice the lemongrass into rounds until you reach the very tough upper stalk. Discard the upper stalk. Transfer the sliced lemongrass to a food processor fitted with the metal chopping blade. Pulse about 12 times, until the lemongrass is finely minced. Measure 1½ tablespoons of the minced lemongrass. (The remaining lemongrass can be frozen for up to 3 months.)

5. Combine the minced lemongrass, ground chicken, shallots, fish sauce, cornstarch, chile, garlic, brown sugar, and salt in a large bowl and mix well. Cover and refrigerate for at least 15 minutes or up to 4 hours. Using your wet hands rinsed under cold water, shape the meat mixture into 12 equal meatballs.

6. Prepare a medium-hot fire in an outdoor grill.

7. To grill the meatballs with a basket, lightly oil the molds (a pump oil sprayer works best). Place the meatballs in the basket and close it. Place the basket on the cooking grate and cover. Grill the meatballs until the undersides are lightly browned, about 4 minutes. Flip the basket over and grill until the other sides are lightly browned and the meatballs are cooked through, about 4 minutes. Remove the meatballs from the basket and transfer to a bowl.

To grill the meatballs without the basket, lightly oil the cooking grate. Place the meatballs on the grill and cover. Grill until

*the undersides are lightly browned, about 4
minutes. Flip the meatballs and cook until the
other sides are browned and the meatballs
are cooked through, about 4 minutes more.
Transfer to a bowl.*

8. Pour the dipping sauce into 4 ramekins.
Divide the rice vermicelli among 4 deep bowls.
Top each with 3 meatballs and equal amounts
of the scallion oil. Serve with the dipping
sauce.

bbq pork meatballs with sweet and spicy barbecue sauce

sweet and spicy bbq sauce

2 tablespoons unsalted butter

1 small yellow onion, finely chopped

2 cloves garlic, minced

2 (12-ounce) bottles ketchup-style chili sauce

¼ cup unsulfured molasses

¼ cup cider vinegar

2 tablespoons Worcestershire sauce

2 tablespoons spicy brown mustard

½ teaspoon hot red pepper sauce

½ teaspoon liquid hickory smoke flavoring (optional)

bbq pork meatballs

1 pound ground pork

⅓ cup dried plain bread crumbs

1 large egg, beaten

¼ cup minced yellow onion

2 tablespoons Sweet and Spicy BBQ Sauce

2 cloves garlic, crushed through a garlic press

1 teaspoon kosher salt

½ teaspoon freshly ground black pepper

These juicy grilled balls began as a filling for the BBQ Pork Meatballs Sandwich on page 51. However, it was hard not to nibble on the meatballs while assembling the sandwiches, and I soon started serving them on their own, usually with baked beans and hot-from-the-oven cornbread. I suppose you could use bottled barbecue sauce, but once you make your own, you'll never go back to the super-sweet supermarket variety. Make the sauce first so it has time to cool, as it is an ingredient in the meatball mixture.

1. To make the barbecue sauce, heat the butter in a heavy-bottomed, medium saucepan over medium heat. Add the onion and cook, stirring occasionally, until golden, about 5 minutes. Stir in the garlic and cook until fragrant, about 1 minute. Stir in the chili sauce, molasses, vinegar, Worcestershire sauce, and mustard and bring to a simmer. Reduce the heat to low and simmer, stirring often, until the sauce is slightly reduced, about 20 minutes. Remove from the heat and stir in the hot sauce and smoke flavoring. Let cool completely. Transfer 1 cup of the barbecue sauce to a bowl and set aside. (The remaining barbecue sauce can be covered and refrigerated for up to 1 month.)

2. To make the meatballs, combine the ground pork, bread crumbs, egg, onion, barbecue sauce, garlic, salt, and pepper together in a large bowl and mix well. Cover and refrigerate for at least 15 minutes or up to 4 hours.

3. Prepare a medium-hot fire in an outdoor grill. Using your wet hands rinsed under cold water, shape the meat mixture into 12 equal meatballs.

4. To grill the meatballs with a basket, lightly oil the molds (a pump oil sprayer works best). Place the meatballs in the basket and close it. Place the basket on the cooking grate and cover. Grill the meatballs until the undersides are lightly browned, about 3 minutes. Flip the basket over and grill until the other sides are lightly browned, about 3 minutes more. Remove the meatballs from the basket. Return the meatballs to the grill and brush with some of the sauce. Grill, turning and brushing with more sauce, until glazed and cooked through, about 2 minutes. Transfer to a platter.

To grill the meatballs without the basket, lightly oil the cooking grate. Place the meatballs on the grill and cover. Grill until the undersides are lightly browned, about 3 minutes. Flip the meatballs and brown the other sides, about 3 minutes. Brush with some of the sauce. Grill, turning and brushing with more sauce, until glazed and cooked through, about 2 minutes. Transfer to a platter.

5. Serve the meatballs hot, with the reserved barbecue sauce in the bowl passed on the side.

grilled salmon meatballs with iceberg wedges and green goddess sauce

makes **4** servings

green goddess sauce

1 tablespoon fresh
lemon juice

½ teaspoon anchovy paste

1 cup mayonnaise

1 scallion, minced

2 tablespoons minced
fresh parsley

2 teaspoons minced
fresh tarragon

Freshly ground black pepper

These pale pink balls with their green sauce are as attractive as they are delicious. Served with a cool chunk of iceberg lettuce and cherry tomatoes, they make a swell lunch, brunch, or supper dish. Use your favorite wild salmon, as there aren't a lot of strong seasonings and the fish's flavor will predominate.

1. To make the sauce, whisk the lemon juice and anchovy paste in a bowl to dissolve the anchovy paste. Add the mayonnaise, scallion, parsley, and tarragon and whisk to combine. Season with pepper. Cover and refrigerate for at least 30 minutes or up to 2 days before serving.

2. To make the meatballs, pulse the salmon in a food processor fitted with the metal chopping blade until finely chopped. Add the panko, scallion, mayonnaise, mustard, salt, and pepper and pulse until combined. Transfer to a bowl, cover, and refrigerate for at least 15 minutes or up to 2 hours.

3. Prepare a medium-hot fire in an outdoor grill. Using hands rinsed under cold water, shape the salmon mixture into 12 equal meatballs.

4. To grill the meatballs with the basket, lightly oil the molds (a pump sprayer works best). Place the meatballs in the basket and close it. Place the basket on the cooking grate and cover.

salmon meatballs

1 pound skinless salmon
fillets, cut into 1-inch chunks

½ cup panko (Japanese
bread crumbs)

1 scallion, minced

2 tablespoons mayonnaise

2 teaspoons Dijon mustard

¾ teaspoon kosher salt

¼ teaspoon freshly ground
black pepper

1 small head iceberg lettuce,
cored and cut into 4 wedges

2 cups cherry tomatoes,
cut into halves

Chopped fresh parsley,
for garnish

Grill the meatballs until the undersides are lightly browned, about 3 minutes. Flip the basket over and grill until the other sides are lightly browned, about 3 minutes more. Remove the meatballs from the basket. Transfer to a platter.

To grill the meatballs without the basket, lightly oil the cooking grate. Place the meatballs on the grill and cover. Grill until the undersides are lightly browned, about 3 minutes. Flip the meatballs and grill until the other sides are lightly browned, about 3 minutes. Transfer to a platter.

5. To serve, divide the iceberg wedges and tomatoes among 4 dinner plates. Add 3 salmon meatballs to each and drizzle generously with the sauce. Sprinkle with the parsley and serve at once.

curried koftas with tomato raita

makes **4** servings

tomato raita

2 plum tomatoes, seeded
and cut into ½-inch dice

½ teaspoon kosher salt

1 cup plain yogurt

1 scallion, minced

2 tablespoons minced
fresh cilantro or mint

curried koftas

1 pound ground lamb

½ cup fresh bread crumbs,
such as from naan or pita

1 large egg, beaten

2 tablespoons chopped
fresh cilantro

1½ teaspoons kosher salt

1 teaspoon Madras-style
curry powder

⅛ teaspoon cayenne pepper

When a country has as many cooks as India, one could probably write a cookbook dedicated to just *kofta* recipes. They are most often braised in a sauce that reflects the flavors of the particular region (such as Lamb Meatballs in Green Curry Sauce on page 90), but here the spicy balls are grilled and served with a separately prepared yogurt *raita*. You can also use all ground round, or a combination of half ground round and half ground lamb, for these meatballs.

1. To make the raita, toss the tomatoes and salt together in a colander. Let stand in the sink to drain for about 30 minutes. Transfer to a small bowl. Add the yogurt, scallion, and cilantro. Cover and let stand to blend the flavors, at least 1 hour or up to 4 hours, or refrigerate for up to 1 day.

2. To make the meatballs, mix the ground lamb, bread crumbs, egg, cilantro, salt, curry powder, and cayenne together with your hands in a large bowl. Cover and refrigerate for at least 15 minutes or up to 4 hours.

3. Prepare a medium-hot fire in an outdoor grill. Using your wet hands rinsed under cold water, shape the mixture into 12 equal meatballs.

4. To grill the meatballs with a basket, lightly spray the molds with oil (a pump oil sprayer works best). Place the meatballs in the basket and close it. Place the basket on the cooking grate and cover. Grill the meatballs until the undersides are lightly browned, about 3 minutes. Flip the basket over and grill until the other sides

are lightly browned and the meatballs are medium-rare, about 3 minutes more. Remove the meatballs from the basket. Transfer to a platter.

To grill the meatballs without the basket, lightly oil the cooking grate. Place the meatballs on the grill and cover. Grill until the undersides are lightly browned, about 3 minutes. Flip the meatballs and grill until the other sides are lightly browned and the meatballs are medium-rare, about 3 minutes. Transfer to a platter.

5. Serve the meatballs hot, with the *raita* passed on the side.

curried kofta sandwiches: Grill 4 naan or other 7-inch-wide flatbreads on the grill, turning occasionally, until heated through, about 1½ minutes. Cut the meatballs into thick slices. Place each naan on a plate. Divide the sliced meatballs among the naan. Top with a handful of baby spinach or shredded romaine lettuce and a large spoonful of *raita*. To eat, fold the naan into a curved taco shape.

MEATBALLS AROUND THE WORLD

As soon as cooks discovered that chopping tough meat was an effective tenderizer, it probably didn't take long for the meat to be rolled into balls for easy eating. Also, the ground meat could be extended with bread crumbs or other fillers to make more servings. No wonder every cuisine in the world has meatballs, and not just one recipe. It is said that there are over 200 kinds of Turkish meatballs! Here is a list of some countries and their names for meatballs.

Albania	*qofte*
Armenia	*kufta*
Austria	*Fleischlaibchen, Fleischlaberl*
Belgium	*ballekes, bouletten*
Denmark	*frikadeller*
Finland	*lihapallat*
Germany	*Fridakelle, Fleischpflanzerl, Bulette, Klopse*
Greece	*keftédes, yuvarlákia*
Hungary	*fasirt, fasirozott*
India	*kofta*
Indonesia	*bakso*
Iran	*kufte,kofteh*
Italy	*polpette*
Netherlands	*gehaktbal*
Norway	*kjøttkaker, kjøttboller*
Philippines	*almondigas, bola-bola*
Poland	*pulpety, klopsiki*
Portugal/Brazil	*almôndegas*
Romania	*chiftele, pârjoale*
Spain/Latin America	*albóndigas*
Sweden	*köttbullar*
Thailand	*look chin*
Vietnam	*thit viên*

balkan ćevapčići with ajvar

ajvar

1 large eggplant

2 medium red bell peppers

2 tablespoons fresh
lemon juice

1 tablespoon minced
fresh parsley

1 clove garlic, minced

⅓ cup extra virgin olive oil

Kosher salt and freshly
ground black pepper

ćevapčići

1 pound ground round
(85 percent lean)

8 ounces ground lamb

8 ounces ground pork

2 cloves garlic, crushed
through a press

2¼ teaspoons kosher salt

1 teaspoon freshly ground
black pepper

I am grateful to my friend Carolyn Bánfalvi and her Hungarian husband, Gabor, for their authentic recipe for *ćevapčići* (pronounced "say-vah-PEE-chee"), grilled elongated meatballs. (Are these technically meatballs? I say that they are made of ground meat, and close enough, and you will be happy you have the recipe!) The name means "little kebabs," even though they aren't always cooked on skewers. They date back to the Ottoman Turkish occupation of Eastern Europe, and are especially popular in the Balkans. Depending on the location and religious restrictions on pork, the kind of meat varies—this version uses a trio of beef, lamb, and pork. The Banfalvis like their *ćevapčići* seasoned with no more than garlic, salt, and pepper. Serve it with *ajvar*, a roasted red pepper and eggplant dip.

1. Prepare a medium-hot fire in an outdoor grill.

2. To make the *ajvar,* place the eggplant and bell peppers on the grill and cover. Grill, turning occasionally, until the pepper skins are black and blistered, about 10 minutes. Transfer to a bowl. Continue grilling and turning the eggplant until the skin is black and blistered and the eggplant feels tender, 5 to 10 minutes more. Transfer to another bowl. Let the vegetables cool.

3. Discard the skins and seeds from the peppers and coarsely chop the flesh. Scoop the softened flesh out of the eggplant skin, discarding the skin. Combine the peppers and eggplant in a food processor fitted with the chopping blade. Add the lemon juice, parsley, and garlic. With the machine running, add the oil and process until pureed. Transfer to a serving bowl and season with salt and pepper. Set aside. (The *ajvar* can be made up to 3 days ahead, covered, and refrigerated. Bring to room temperature before serving.)

4. To make the *ćevapčići*, combine the ground round, ground lamb, ground pork, garlic, salt, and pepper in a large bowl and mix well. Cover and refrigerate for at least 15 minutes or up to 4 hours. Using your wet hands rinsed under cold water, shape into 24 equal sausages, about 1 inch wide and 2½ inches long. Place on a baking sheet, cover loosely with plastic wrap and refrigerate for at least 15 minutes or up to 4 hours.

5. Build another fire in the grill, if necessary. Oil the cooking grate. Place the *ćevapčići* meatballs on the grill and cover. Grill, turning often, until nicely browned and cooked through, about 6 minutes. Transfer to a platter. Serve hot, with the *ajvar.*

meatballs
and pasta

beef lovers' ziti
and fresh beef meatballs

makes **4** to **6** servings

fresh beef meatballs

1½ pounds boneless beef flanken or chuck, cut into 1-inch chunks

1 cup fresh bread crumbs

¼ cup hearty red wine, such as Shiraz

2 large eggs, beaten

1 medium yellow onion, shredded on the large holes of a box grater

1 clove garlic, crushed through a press

3 tablespoons chopped fresh parsley

1¾ teaspoons kosher salt

½ teaspoon freshly ground black pepper

Many meatballs have a combination of meats, but these are made with beef alone. Boneless beef flanken has wonderful flavor, but it can be pricey so I often opt for chuck. The minor effort needed to grind the beef at home will transform a familiar dish into something extraordinary, but it is also worth making with store-bought ground round.

1. To make the meatballs, spread the beef on a baking sheet and freeze until partially frozen, 30 minutes to 1 hour. In batches, transfer the beef to a food processor fitted with the chopping blade. Pulse about 12 times, until the beef is coarsely ground—the pieces should be less than ⅛ inch square. Transfer the ground beef to a medium bowl.

2. Combine the bread crumbs and wine in a small bowl. Let stand until the crumbs soften, about 3 minutes. Return the beef to the food processor. Add the soaked crumbs, eggs, onion, garlic, parsley, salt, and pepper. Pulse a few times until the beef is ground a bit more finely and the ingredients are combined. Return to the bowl, cover, and refrigerate for at least 15 minutes or up to 4 hours.

3. To make the sauce, heat the oil in a Dutch oven over medium heat. Add the onion and celery and cook, stirring occasionally, until softened but not browned, about 5 minutes. Stir in the garlic and cook until fragrant, about 1 minute. Add the wine and bring to a boil. Stir in the tomatoes, beef broth, rosemary, thyme, bay leaf,

beefy pasta sauce

2 tablespoons olive oil

1 medium yellow onion, chopped

1 medium celery rib with leaves, chopped

2 cloves garlic, finely chopped

½ cup hearty red wine, such as Shiraz

1 (28-ounce) can tomatoes in puree, chopped

1 cup homemade beef stock or canned reduced-sodium beef broth

1 teaspoon dried rosemary

½ teaspoon dried thyme

1 bay leaf

½ teaspoon crushed hot red pepper

3 tablespoons olive oil

1 pound ziti, rigatoni, or other tubular pasta

Ricotta cheese, at room temperature, for serving

Freshly grated Parmesan cheese, for serving

and hot pepper. Bring to a simmer over medium-high heat. Reduce the heat to medium-low and simmer for 30 minutes.

4. Meanwhile, using your wet hands rinsed under cold water, shape the meat mixture into 18 equal meatballs. Transfer to a baking sheet. Heat the 3 tablespoons of olive oil in a large nonstick skillet over medium heat. In batches, add the meatballs. Cook, turning occasionally, until lightly browned on all sides, about 6 minutes. Return the browned meatballs to the baking sheet. Pour off the fat, but not the browned bits, from the skillet. Return to medium heat. Add ½ cup water and bring to a boil, scraping up the browned bits in the skillet. Stir into the sauce. Add the meatballs to the sauce and cover with the lid ajar. Simmer until the meatballs are cooked through, about 30 minutes.

5. Meanwhile, bring a large pot of salted water to a boil over high heat. Add the ziti and cook according to the package directions until al dente. Drain well and return to the pot.

6. Using a slotted spoon, transfer the meatballs to a platter. Remove the bay leaf from the sauce and discard. Add the sauce to the ziti in the pot and stir well. Transfer to a large warmed serving bowl and top with the meatballs. Spoon into bowls and top each serving with a dollop of ricotta. Serve hot, with Parmesan passed on the side.

checkered tablecloth
spaghetti and meatballs

makes to servings

meatballs

2 tablespoons olive oil

1 large onion, finely chopped

2 cloves garlic, minced

1 pound ground round
(85 percent lean)

1 pound sweet Italian
sausage, casings removed

1 cup dried plain bread
crumbs

½ cup freshly grated
Parmesan cheese

2 large eggs, beaten

1 teaspoon dried oregano

1 teaspoon dried basil

¾ teaspoon salt

¼ teaspoon freshly ground
black pepper

classic tomato pasta sauce

2 tablespoons olive oil

1 medium yellow onion,
chopped

2 cloves garlic, minced

1 (28-ounce) can crushed
tomatoes

1 (16-ounce) can tomato
sauce

1 cup hearty red wine,
such as Shiraz

2 teaspoons dried oregano

2 teaspoons dried basil

¼ teaspoon crushed
hot red pepper

1 bay leaf

1½ pounds spaghetti

Freshly grated Parmesan
cheese, for serving

A composite of what I've learned about spaghetti and meatballs from the various Italian grandmothers in my life, this is everything that the classic dish should be—the perfect example of *abbondanza*, which means glorious excess. This makes a large amount, but even if you don't have a big family, make the entire amount to have leftovers for another meal. In the old days, the meatballs would be fried in oil, but most cooks I know prefer to bake them to keep the stovetop clean of splatters.

1. To make the meatballs, heat the oil in a medium skillet over medium heat. Add the onion and cook, stirring occasionally, until golden, about 5 minutes. Add the garlic and cook until fragrant, about 1 minute more. Transfer to a large bowl and let cool completely.

2. Add the ground round, sausage, bread crumbs, Parmesan, eggs,

oregano, basil, salt, and pepper to the onion mixture and mix well. Cover and refrigerate for at least 15 minutes or up to 4 hours.

3. Position a rack in the center of the oven and preheat to 375°F. Lightly oil a large metal roasting pan. Using your wet hands rinsed under cold water, shape the meat mixture into 24 equal meatballs. Arrange the meatballs in the pan. Bake until lightly browned, about 25 minutes.

4. Meanwhile, start the sauce. Heat the oil in a heavy-bottomed nonreactive pot over medium heat. Add the onion and cook, stirring occasionally, until golden, about 5 minutes. Stir in the garlic and cook until fragrant, about 1 minute more. Stir in the tomatoes, tomato sauce, wine, oregano, basil, hot pepper, and bay leaf. Bring to a simmer over high heat. Reduce the heat to medium-low and simmer, uncovered and stirring occasionally, for 30 minutes.

5. Transfer the meatballs to a platter. Pour the fat out of the roasting pan, leaving the browned bits in the pan. Heat the pan over high heat. When it sizzles, pour in ½ cup water and bring to a boil, scraping up the browned bits in the pan with a wooden spatula. Stir into the sauce. Add the meatballs to the sauce and return to a simmer. Cook, stirring occasionally, until the meatballs are cooked through, about 30 minutes more.

6. Meanwhile, bring a large pot of salted water to a boil over high heat. Add the spaghetti and cook according to the package directions until al dente. Drain well and return to the pot.

7. Using a slotted spoon, transfer the meatballs to a platter. Remove the bay leaf from the sauce and discard. Add the sauce to the spaghetti in the pot and stir well. Transfer the spaghetti and sauce to a large warmed serving bowl and top with the meatballs. Serve hot, with Parmesan passed at the table.

sicilian meatballs: My friend Marguerite Scandiffio adds ½ cup chopped raisins and ⅓ cup toasted and cooled pine nuts to the meatball mixture.

old world meatballs
with everyday tomato sauce

everyday tomato sauce

2 tablespoons olive oil

1 medium yellow onion, chopped

2 cloves garlic, finely chopped

1 (28-ounce) can tomato puree

½ cup hearty red wine, such as Shiraz

2 teaspoons dried oregano

1 teaspoon dried basil

¼ teaspoon crushed hot red pepper

1 bay leaf

old world meatballs

1½ cups fresh bread crumbs

½ cup milk

1½ pounds ground round (85 percent lean)

8 ounces lean ground pork

1 cup finely chopped onion

⅔ cup (about 3 ounces) freshly grated Pecorino Romano cheese

¼ cup finely chopped parsley

1 large egg, beaten

Grated zest of 1 lemon

1 clove garlic, minced

1 teaspoon salt

½ teaspoon freshly ground black pepper

⅛ teaspoon freshly ground nutmeg

1 pound spaghetti

Freshly grated Pecorino Romano cheese, for serving

I often swap recipes with my dear friend, cookbook author and cooking teacher Diane Phillips. Here is her grandmother Aleandra's recipe for *polpette*, and a special one it is, too. Flavored with lemon zest and sharp Romano cheese, these are flavorful enough to be fried and served without sauce. Aleandra never fried her meatballs if they were going to be served with pasta, but simmered them directly in the sauce.

1. To make the sauce, heat the oil in a large saucepan over medium heat. Add the onion and cook, stirring occasionally, until softened, about 5 minutes. Stir in the garlic and cook until fragrant, about 1 minute. Stir in the tomato puree, wine, oregano, basil, hot pepper, and bay leaf. Bring to a simmer. Reduce the heat to low and simmer, stirring occasionally, until the sauce is slightly reduced, about 45 minutes. Remove and discard the bay leaf. Makes about 3½ cups.

2. Meanwhile, make the meatballs. Stir the bread crumbs and milk together in a large bowl and let stand until the crumbs soak up the milk, about 3 minutes. Add the beef, pork, onion, Romano, parsley, egg, lemon zest, garlic, salt, pepper, and nutmeg and mix well. Cover and refrigerate for at least 15 minutes or up to 4 hours. Using your wet hands rinsed under cold water, shape into 24 equal meatballs. Transfer to a baking sheet.

3. Carefully add the meatballs to the simmering tomato sauce. Cook, stirring occasionally and adding more water if the sauce gets too thick, until the meatballs are cooked through, about 1 hour.

4. Meanwhile, bring a large pot of salted water to a boil over high heat. Add the spaghetti and cook according to the package directions until al dente. Drain well and return to the pot.

5. Using a slotted spoon, transfer the meatballs to a platter. Remove the bay leaf from the sauce and discard. Add the sauce to the spaghetti in the pot and stir well. Transfer the spaghetti and sauce to a large warmed serving bowl and top with the meatballs. Serve hot, with Romano passed at the table.

SPAGHETTI AND MEATBALLS

Many food lovers consider the Italian-American classic spaghetti and meatballs the ultimate meatball dish. Just as chop suey and General Tso's chicken were American creations but are mainstays on Chinese restaurant menus, few Italian nationals would recognize our spaghetti and meatballs. Red meat was scarce in most of Italy, so *polpette* were reserved for very special occasions, carefully formed into small balls and used as a component in baked dishes such as lasagna. If meatballs intended for a less formal meal were simmered in a sauce, the sauce was used to coat pasta and served as a first course, with the meatballs presented separately as an entrée. Recipes in contemporary Italian cookbooks for spaghetti and meatballs were influenced by the twentieth-century American version.

fusilli with veal meatballs
and marsala-mushroom sauce

makes to 6 servings

veal meatballs

1 cup fresh bread crumbs

¼ cup milk

1½ pounds ground veal

2 large eggs, beaten

¼ cup minced shallots

2 tablespoons chopped
fresh parsley

1½ teaspoons kosher salt

½ teaspoon freshly ground
black pepper

Marsala, mushrooms, and veal are old pals, and come together in many Italian dishes. It was a natural progression to turn them into a meatball sauce for twisty fusilli pasta. Use dry Marsala, and save the sweet version for making desserts.

1. To make the meatballs, stir the bread crumbs and milk together in a large bowl and let stand until the crumbs soak up the milk, about 3 minutes. Add the veal, eggs, shallots, parsley, salt, and pepper. Cover and refrigerate for at least 15 minutes or up to 4 hours. Using your wet hands rinsed under cold water, shape into 18 equal meatballs. Transfer to a baking sheet.

2. To make the sauce, melt the butter in a large skillet over medium heat. Add the mushrooms and cook, stirring often, until beginning to brown, about 7 minutes. Stir in the shallots and cook until they soften, about 2 minutes. Sprinkle in the flour and stir well. Add the Marsala and bring to a boil. Stir in the broth and cream and return to a boil.

3. Carefully add the meatballs to the sauce and return to a simmer. Reduce the heat to medium-low and cover. Simmer until the meatballs are cooked through, about 20 minutes. Season the sauce with salt and pepper.

marsala-mushroom sauce

2 tablespoons unsalted butter

10 ounces cremini mushrooms, thinly sliced

2 tablespoons minced shallots

3 tablespoons all-purpose flour

½ cup dry Marsala

1¾ cups homemade beef stock or canned reduced-sodium beef broth

⅓ cup heavy cream

Kosher salt and freshly ground black pepper

1 pound fusilli, fettuccine, or spaghetti

Chopped fresh parsley, for garnish

Freshly grated Parmesan cheese, for serving

4. Meanwhile, bring a large pot of salted water to a boil over high heat. Add the fusilli and cook according to the package directions until al dente. Drain well and return to the pot.

5. Using a slotted spoon, carefully transfer the meatballs to a platter (they are more delicate than most meatballs). Add the sauce to the fusilli in the pot and stir well. Transfer the fusilli and sauce to a large warmed serving bowl, top with the meatballs, and garnish with parsley. Serve hot, with Parmesan passed at the table.

spaghetti with three-meat meatballs bolognese

three-meat meatballs

3 tablespoons olive oil

1 medium yellow onion, finely chopped

2 cloves garlic, minced

¾ cup fresh bread crumbs

⅓ cup whole milk

1½ pounds meat loaf mix, or 8 ounces each ground round, ground pork, and ground veal

1 large egg, beaten

2 tablespoons chopped fresh parsley

1¼ teaspoons kosher salt

1 teaspoon dried oregano

½ teaspoon freshly ground black pepper

If I had to choose my favorite pasta-and-meatball recipe, this might be the winner. The combination of beef (assertive flavor), pork (juiciness from its fat), and veal (cohesiveness from its collagen) makes terrific meatballs. And the creamy, vegetable-flecked sauce is comforting and sophisticated at the same time.

1. To make the meatballs, heat the oil in a medium nonstick skillet over medium heat. Add the onion and cook, stirring occasionally, until translucent, about 5 minutes. Stir in the garlic and cook until fragrant, about 1 minute. Transfer to a large bowl and let cool.

2. Combine the bread crumbs and milk in a small bowl and let stand until the bread soaks up the milk, about 3 minutes. Drain in a wire sieve and press on the crumbs to remove the excess milk. Transfer to the bowl. Add the meat loaf mix, egg, parsley, salt, oregano, and pepper and mix well. Cover and refrigerate for at least 15 minutes or up to 4 hours.

3. To make the sauce, melt the butter in a Dutch oven or covered casserole over medium heat. Add the onion, carrot, and celery. Cook, stirring occasionally, until softened, about 5 minutes. Stir in the garlic and cook until fragrant, about 1 minute. Add the wine and bring to a boil. Stir in the tomatoes, tomato paste, oregano, and basil. Bring to a simmer. Reduce the heat to medium-low. Simmer, uncovered and stirring occasionally, for 30 minutes.

bolognese sauce

2 tablespoons unsalted butter

1 small yellow onion, finely chopped

1 small carrot, finely chopped

1 small celery rib, finely chopped

2 cloves garlic, minced

½ cup dry white wine, such as Pinot Grigio

1 (28-ounce) can crushed tomatoes

2 tablespoons tomato paste

1 teaspoon dried oregano

1 teaspoon dried basil

½ cup heavy cream

Kosher salt and freshly ground black pepper

1 pound spaghetti

Freshly grated Parmesan cheese, for serving

4. Position a rack in the center of the oven and preheat to 375°F. Lightly oil a metal roasting pan. Using your wet hands rinsed under cold water, shape the meat mixture into 18 equal meatballs and place in the pan. Bake until the meatballs are browned, about 25 minutes.

5. Transfer the browned meatballs to a platter. Pour off and discard the fat, but not the browned bits, in the pan. Place the pan over high heat. When the pan sizzles, add ½ cup water to the pan and bring to a boil, scraping up the browned bits with a wooden spatula. Boil until reduced by half, about 2 minutes. Stir into the sauce. Add the meatballs and simmer until the sauce is lightly thickened, about 30 minutes more. During the last 5 minutes of cooking, stir in the cream and season with salt and pepper.

6. Meanwhile, bring a large pot of lightly salted water to a boil over high heat. Add the spaghetti and cook according to the package directions until al dente. Drain and return to the pot.

7. Using a slotted spoon, transfer the meatballs to a platter. Add the sauce to the spaghetti in the pot and mix. Transfer to a warmed serving bowl. Top with the meatballs and serve hot, with Parmesan passed on the side.

ziti with sausage meatballs and broccolini

sausage meatballs

¾ cup fresh bread crumbs

⅓ cup whole milk

12 ounces sweet Italian pork sausage, casings removed

8 ounces ground pork

1 small onion, shredded on the large holes of a box grater

1 large egg, beaten

¼ teaspoon kosher salt

⅛ teaspoon freshly ground black pepper

1 pound ziti, rigatoni, or other tubular pasta

2 tablespoons extra virgin olive oil

2 cloves garlic, thinly sliced

½ teaspoon anchovy paste

1 pound broccolini (about 2 bunches), cut into 2-inch lengths

1 cup canned reduced-sodium chicken broth

¼ teaspoon crushed hot red pepper

½ cup (2 ounces) freshly grated Parmesan cheese, plus more for serving

Salt

I used to make this with broccoli rabe, until I realized that I just don't like that vegetable's bitterness. Then I discovered broccolini, a relatively new addition to the produce department that has more slender stalks and is much "sweeter" than its cousin. Here it is put to use with sausage meatballs in a garlicky sauce for sturdy ziti.

1. To make the meatballs, position a rack in the center of the oven and preheat to 375°F. Lightly oil a rimmed baking sheet.

2. Soak the bread crumbs in the milk in a medium bowl until softened, about 3 minutes. Add the sausage, ground pork, onion, egg, salt, and pepper and mix well to combine. Cover and refrigerate for at least 15 minutes or up to 4 hours.

3. Using your wet hands rinsed under cold water, shape the sausage mixture into 18 equal meatballs. Arrange on the baking sheet. Bake until browned and the meatballs are cooked through, about 30 minutes. Remove from the oven.

4. Meanwhile, bring a large pot of lightly salted water to a boil over high heat. Add the ziti and cook according to the package directions until al dente. Drain well. Return the ziti to the pot.

5. While the pasta is cooking, combine the oil and garlic in a large skillet over medium heat. Cook, stirring often, until the garlic is golden but not browned, about 2 minutes. Stir in the anchovy paste. Add the broccolini and stir well. Add the meatballs, broth, and hot pepper. Cover and cook, stirring occasionally, until the broccolini is tender, about 5 minutes.

6. Add the broccolini mixture to the ziti in the pot. Add the Parmesan and mix well. Season with salt. Serve hot, with additional Parmesan passed on the side.

fettuccine with veal-ricotta meatballs and fresh basil and tomato sauce

makes to servings

fresh basil and tomato sauce

2 tablespoons unsalted butter

1 medium yellow onion, finely chopped

1 clove garlic, minced

2½ pounds ripe plum tomatoes, peeled, seeded, and chopped in a food processor, or 1 (28-ounce) can crushed tomatoes

½ cup dry white wine, such as Pinot Grigio

Kosher salt and freshly ground black pepper

⅓ cup chopped fresh basil

veal-ricotta meatballs

½ cup fresh bread crumbs

¼ cup milk

1 pound ground veal

⅓ cup ricotta cheese

2 tablespoons freshly grated Parmesan cheese

1 large egg yolk, beaten

1 teaspoon kosher salt

¼ teaspoon freshly ground black pepper

1 pound fresh fettuccine

Freshly grated Parmesan cheese, for serving

Meatballs are not always hefty and spicy. Veal and ricotta, two gently flavored foods, are the main ingredients here. The resulting meatballs and the basil-scented sauce are delicate enough to be served with fresh pasta. In fact, this is one pasta and meatball dish that I serve with white wine. Wait until the tomatoes are at their seasonal peak, or use canned tomatoes. Try the meatballs without the pasta as an appetizer.

1. To make the sauce, melt the butter in a large saucepan over medium heat. Add the onion and cook, stirring occasionally, until tender, about 5 minutes. Stir in the garlic and cook until fragrant, about 1 minute. Stir in the tomatoes and wine and cover with the lid ajar. Bring to a simmer. Reduce the heat to medium-low and simmer, stirring occasionally, until the tomato juices have thickened, about 45 minutes.

2. Meanwhile, make the meatballs. Stir the bread crumbs and milk together in a large bowl and let stand until the crumbs soak up the milk, about 3 minutes. Add the veal, ricotta, Parmesan, egg yolk, salt, and pepper. Cover and refrigerate for at least 15 minutes or up to 4 hours. Using your wet hands rinsed under cold water, shape into 18 equal meatballs. Transfer to a baking sheet.

3. Stir the basil into the sauce. Carefully add the meatballs to the sauce. Cook, stirring occasionally and adding water if the sauce gets too thick, until the meatballs are cooked through, about 1 hour.

4. Meanwhile, bring a large pot of salted water to a boil over high heat. Add the fettuccine and cook according to the package directions until al dente. Drain well and return to the pot.

5. Using a slotted spoon, carefully transfer the meatballs to a platter (they are more delicate than most meatballs). Add the sauce to the fettuccine in the pot and stir well. Transfer the fettuccine and sauce to a large warmed serving bowl and top with the meatballs. Serve hot, with Parmesan passed at the table.

bucatini with fresh pork meatballs amatriciana

makes to servings

fresh pork meatballs

1½ pounds boneless pork butt, cut into 1-inch chunks

1 cup fresh bread crumbs

½ cup whole milk

2 large eggs, beaten

1 medium yellow onion, shredded on the large holes of a box grater

2 cloves garlic, crushed through a press

2 teaspoons finely chopped fresh oregano, or 1 teaspoon dried oregano

1¾ teaspoons kosher salt

¼ teaspoon crushed hot red pepper

3 tablespoons olive oil

amatriciana sauce

4 ounces sliced and coarsely chopped pancetta

2 tablespoons olive oil

3 cloves garlic, finely chopped

1 (28-ounce) can crushed tomatoes

2 tablespoons tomato paste

1 tablespoon chopped fresh oregano, or 2 teaspoons dried oregano

½ teaspoon crushed hot red pepper

1 pound bucatini or spaghetti

Freshly grated Pecorino Romano cheese, for serving

Pork-infused, and boldly flavored with garlic and peppers, *Amatriciana* sauce is considered a Roman specialty, even if it isn't exactly local (it probably gets its name from Amatrice, which is about 80 miles from Rome). It is usually served without meatballs, but they are a natural addition. You can certainly make the meatballs with supermarket ground pork, but when a dish is this special, I go to the minor effort of chopping the meat at home in a food processor.

1. To make the pork meatballs, spread the pork on a baking sheet and freeze until partially frozen, 30 minutes to 1 hour. In batches, transfer to a food processor fitted with the chopping blade. Pulse about 12 times, until the pork is coarsely ground—the pieces should be less than ⅛ inch square.

2. Combine the bread crumbs and milk in a small bowl. Let stand until the crumbs soften, about 3 minutes. Drain in a wire sieve and press lightly to extract the excess milk. Add the soaked crumbs, eggs, onion, garlic, oregano, salt, and hot pepper. Pulse a few times until the pork is ground a bit more finely and the ingredients are combined. Transfer to a bowl, cover, and refrigerate for at least 15 minutes or up to 4 hours.

3. To make the sauce, combine the pancetta and oil in a heavy-bottomed pot over medium heat. Cook, stirring often, until the pancetta is lightly browned, about 10 minutes. Stir in the garlic and cook until fragrant but not browned, about 30 seconds. Stir in the tomatoes, 1 cup water, the tomato paste, oregano, and hot pepper. Bring to a simmer over medium-high heat. Reduce the heat to medium-low and simmer for 30 minutes.

4. Meanwhile, using your wet hands rinsed under cold water, shape the meat mixture into 18 equal meatballs. Transfer to a baking sheet. Heat the 3 tablespoons of olive oil in a large nonstick skillet over medium heat. In batches, add the meatballs. Cook, turning occasionally, until lightly browned on all sides, about 6 minutes. Return the browned meatballs to the baking sheet. Pour off the fat, but not the browned bits, from the skillet. Return to medium heat. Add ¼ cup water and bring to a boil, scraping up the browned bits in the skillet. Stir into the sauce.

5. Add the meatballs to the sauce and cover with the lid ajar. Simmer until the meatballs are cooked through, about 30 minutes.

6. Meanwhile, bring a large pot of salted water to a boil over high heat. Add the bucatini and cook according to the package directions until al dente. Drain well and return to the pot.

7. Using a slotted spoon, transfer the meatballs to a platter. Add the sauce to the spaghetti in the pot and stir well. Transfer the spaghetti and sauce to a large warmed serving bowl and top with the meatballs. Serve hot, with Romano passed at the table.

holiday meatball lasagna

tomato sauce

2 tablespoons olive oil

1 large yellow onion, chopped

3 cloves garlic, minced

1 cup dry red wine

1 (28-ounce) can tomatoes with added thick puree

2 (6-ounce) cans tomato paste

1 (8-ounce) can tomato sauce

1½ teaspoons dried basil

1 teaspoon dried oregano

¼ teaspoon crushed hot red pepper

meatballs

2 pounds meat loaf mix, or 1 pound ground round, 8 ounces ground pork, and 8 ounces ground veal

¾ cup dried Italian-seasoned bread crumbs

2 large eggs, beaten

1½ teaspoons kosher salt

½ teaspoon freshly ground black pepper

1 pound lasagna noodles

1 (32-ounce) container ricotta cheese

1½ cups (6 ounces) freshly grated Parmesan cheese

2 large eggs, beaten

⅓ cup chopped fresh basil or parsley

1 teaspoon kosher salt

¼ teaspoon freshly ground black pepper

4 cups (1 pound) shredded mozzarella cheese

This is one of the recipes that introduced me to the "when a meatball is more than a meatball" concept. Many of my Italian-American friends serve lasagna every Christmas. But instead of the commonplace dish with ground meat in sauce, it is this refined version, with tiny meatballs lovingly rolled and simmered in the sauce. This sends the clear message that the guests at the table deserve the special effort. Make it in stages, preparing the meatballs and sauce ahead, to streamline the operation.

1. To make the sauce, heat the oil in a Dutch oven or flameproof casserole over medium heat. Add the onion and cook, stirring often, until golden, about 5 minutes. Stir in the garlic and cook until fragrant, about 1 minute. Add the wine and bring to a boil. Stir in the tomatoes with their puree, 1 cup water, the tomato paste, tomato sauce, basil, oregano, and hot pepper. Bring to a boil and reduce the heat to low.

Simmer uncovered, stirring occasionally, until lightly thickened, about 1 hour.

2. To make the meatballs, combine the meat loaf mix, bread crumbs, eggs, salt, and pepper in a large bowl and mix well. Using your wet hands rinsed under cold water, roll into about 32 equal small meatballs. Place on a baking sheet.

3. A few at a time, gently stir the meatballs into the simmering sauce. Return to the simmer and cook, stirring occasionally, until the sauce is thickened and the meatballs are cooked through, about 30 minutes. (The sauce and meatballs can be prepared up to 2 days ahead, cooled, covered and refrigerated, or frozen in airtight containers for up to 1 month.)

4. Meanwhile, bring a large pot of lightly salted water to a boil over high heat. Add the lasagna noodles and cook according to the package directions until al dente. Drain and rinse under cold running water. (The noodles can be prepared up to 2 hours ahead, tossed with 1 tablespoon olive oil, and stored at room temperature.) You may not use all of the noodles, but it is good to have a couple of extras in case of breakage.

5. Position a rack in the center of the oven and preheat to 375°F. Lightly oil a 15 x 10-inch baking dish.

6. Mix the ricotta cheese, 1 cup of the Parmesan, the eggs, basil, salt, and pepper together in a medium bowl.

7. Using a slotted spoon, transfer the meatballs to a bowl. Spread about ½ cup of the tomato sauce in the baking dish. Arrange 5 lasagna noodles (4 horizontally and 1 vertically), slightly overlapping and cut to fit, in the dish. Spread half of the ricotta mixture over the noodles, then sprinkle with 2 cups of the mozzarella. Scatter half of the meatballs over the cheese, then top with one-third of the remaining tomato sauce. Arrange another 5 noodles in the dish. Cover with the remaining ricotta filling, the remaining 2 cups mozzarella, the remaining meatballs, then half of the remaining sauce. Top with another layer of noodles and spread with the remaining tomato sauce. Sprinkle with the remaining ½ cup Parmesan cheese. Cover with aluminum foil. (The lasagna can be prepared up to 1 day ahead, cooled, covered, and refrigerated.)

8. Bake the lasagna for 30 minutes. Remove the foil and bake until bubbling throughout, about 30 minutes more. Let stand for 10 minutes before serving.

turkey meatball and vegetable fricassee with egg noodles

makes to servings

turkey meatballs

2 tablespoons vegetable oil

1 small yellow onion, chopped

1¼ pounds ground turkey

⅔ cup fresh bread crumbs

1 large egg, beaten

½ teaspoon dried thyme

½ teaspoon dried sage

½ teaspoon crumbled dried rosemary

1¼ teaspoons kosher salt

½ teaspoon freshly ground black pepper

sauce

2 tablespoons unsalted butter

1 medium yellow onion, chopped

2 medium carrots, cut into ½-inch dice

2 medium celery ribs, cut into ½-inch dice

3 tablespoons all-purpose flour

2⅓ cups canned reduced-sodium chicken broth

⅓ cup heavy cream or milk

Kosher salt and freshly ground black pepper

1 pound medium-wide egg noodles

Chopped fresh parsley, for garnish

Tender turkey meatballs in a creamy, vegetable-studded sauce served over egg noodles—comfort food doesn't get more comforting than this. I first enjoyed a similar dish, which represents the best of solid American cooking, during a visit to an Amish farmhouse in Pennsylvania. If you wish, substitute one-third of the chicken broth with dry white wine for a fricassee with a French accent.

1. To make the meatballs, heat 1 tablespoon of the oil in a small skillet over medium heat. Add the onion and cook until tender, about 5 minutes. Transfer to a large bowl and let cool slightly. Add the ground turkey, bread crumbs, egg, thyme, sage, rosemary, salt, and pepper and mix well. Cover and refrigerate for at least 15 minutes or up to 4 hours. Using your wet hands rinsed under cold water, shape into 18 equal meatballs and transfer to a baking sheet.

2. Heat the remaining 1 tablespoon oil in a large nonstick skillet over medium heat. In batches, add the meatballs and cook, turning occasionally, until lightly browned, about 6 minutes. Transfer to a plate.

3. To make the sauce, add the butter to the skillet and melt. Add the onion, carrots, and celery and cook, stirring up the browned bits in the skillet with a wooden spatula, until the vegetables soften, about 5 minutes. Sprinkle with the flour and stir well. Stir in the broth and cream and bring to a simmer. Return the meatballs to the skillet and cover with the lid ajar. Reduce the heat to medium-low and simmer until the vegetables are tender and the meatballs are cooked through, about 20 minutes. Season with salt and pepper.

4. Meanwhile, bring a large pot of lightly salted water to a boil over high heat. Add the noodles and cook according to the package directions. Drain well.

5. Serve the noodles in bowls, topped with the fricassee and sprinkled with parsley.

metric conversions and equivalents

Metric Conversion Formulas

TO CONVERT	MULTIPLY
Ounces to grams	Ounces by 28.35
Pounds to kilograms	Pounds by .454
Teaspoons to milliliters	Teaspoons by 4.93
Tablespoons to milliliters	Tablespoons by 14.79
Fluid ounces to milliliters	Fluid ounces by 29.57
Cups to milliliters	Cups by 236.59
Cups to liters	Cups by .236
Pints to liters	Pints by .473
Quarts to liters	Quarts by .946
Gallons to liters	Gallons by 3.785
Inches to centimeters	Inches by 2.54

Approximate Metric Equivalents

VOLUME

¼ teaspoon	1 milliliter
½ teaspoon	2.5 milliliters
¾ teaspoon	4 milliliters
1 teaspoon	5 milliliters
2 teaspoons	10 milliliters
1 tablespoon (½ fluid ounce)	15 milliliters
¼ cup	60 milliliters
⅓ cup	80 milliliters
½ cup (4 fluid ounces)	120 milliliters
⅔ cup	160 milliliters
¾ cup	180 milliliters
1 cup (8 fluid ounces)	240 milliliters
2 cups (1 pint)	460 milliliters
3 cups	700 milliliters
4 cups (1 quart)	.95 liter
1 quart plus ¼ cup	1 liter
4 quarts (1 gallon)	3.8 liters

WEIGHT

¼ ounce	7 grams
½ ounce	14 grams
¾ ounce	21 grams
1 ounce	28 grams
2 ounces	57 grams
3 ounces	85 grams
4 ounces (¼ pound)	113 grams
5 ounces	142 grams
6 ounces	170 grams
7 ounces	198 grams
8 ounces (½ pound)	227 grams
16 ounces (1 pound)	454 grams
35.25 ounces (2.2 pounds)	1 kilogram

LENGTH

¼ inch	6 millimeters
½ inch	1¼ centimeters
1 inch	2½ centimeters
2 inches	5 centimeters
6 inches	15¼ centimeters
12 inches (1 foot)	30 centimeters

Oven Temperatures

To convert Fahrenheit to Celsius, subtract 32 from Fahrenheit, multiply the result by 5, then divide by 9.

Description	Fahrenheit	Celsius	British Gas Mark
Very cool	200°	95°	0
Very cool	225°	110°	¼
Very cool	250°	120°	½
Cool	275°	135°	1
Cool	300°	150°	2
Warm	325°	165°	3
Moderate	350°	175°	4
Moderately hot	375°	190°	5
Fairly hot	400°	200°	6
Hot	425°	220°	7
Very hot	450°	230°	8
Very hot	475°	245°	9

Common Ingredients and Their Approximate Equivalents

1 cup uncooked rice = 225 grams
1 cup all-purpose flour = 140 grams
1 stick butter (4 ounces • ½ cup • 8 tablespoons) = 110 grams
1 cup butter (8 ounces • 2 sticks • 16 tablespoons) = 220 grams
1 cup brown sugar, firmly packed = 225 grams
1 cup granulated sugar = 200 grams

Information compiled from *Recipes into Type* by Joan Whitman and Dolores Simon (Newton, MA: Biscuit Books, 2000); *The New Food Lover's Companion* by Sharon Tyler Herbst (Hauppauge, NY: Barron's, 1995); and *Rosemary Brown's Big Kitchen Instruction Book* (Kansas City, MO: Andrews McMeel, 1998).

index